DOCUMENTS OF MODERN HISTORY

General Editors:

A. G. Dickens
The Director, Institute of Historical Research, University of London

Alun Davies
Professor of Modern History, University College, Swansea

ELIZABETHAN PEOPLE

PEOPLE

STATE AND SOCIETY

edited by

Joel Hurstfield

Astor Professor of English History,
University College, London

and

Alan G. R. Smith

Lecturer in History,
University of Glasgow

Edward Arnold

Printed in Great Britain
by Unwin Brothers Limited
The Gresham Press, Old Woking, Surrey, England
A member of the Staples Printing Group

CONTENTS

II THE ECONOMY

III INTELLECTUAL DEVELOPMENTS

IV RELIGION

V GOVERNMENT AND ADMINISTRATION

PREFACE

Our aim in this volume has been to draw to the fullest upon the enormous variety of sources available to the student of Elizabethan England. This has meant the exploration of official and unofficial records on administration, the economy and religion; but we have used, over a wide area, the literary sources both for their own interest and attraction and as commentaries, by contemporaries, upon the world in which they were living.

When we began work on this book we had no idea of the time it would take and the great amount of work involved in collecting, discarding, sifting; but it has been an immensely pleasurable and instructive task. We hope that our readers will derive from this book some of the pleasure and understanding that it gave to us. We acknowledge a special debt to Mrs. Katie Edwards, of University College, London, who typed this book and whose faithfulness to us, and to the texts, kept pace with our researches and enthusiasm.

J. H.
A. G. R. S.

ACKNOWLEDGEMENTS

The editors and publisher wish to thank the following for their permission to reprint passages from copyright works: Allen and Unwin I,6; G. Bell II,11, V,26(i); Cambridge University Press III,2, III,11, III,29, V,20; *English Historical Review* V,16; the Folger Shakespeare Library, I,19, I,30, II,3, III,1(i)(ii), III,3, III,29, IV,3, IV,12, IV,21, IV,21, IV,22; V,2; the Hakluyt Society I,31, I,32; the Institute of Historical Research III,12, IV,19; the Malone Society III,21; Manchester University Press III,20, III,25; Oliver and Boyd II,19; Penguin I,27, III,24, IV,25; University of Pennsylvania Press I,6, V,10; the Royal Historical Society I,8, I,11, I,15, I,16, II,6; St. Catherine's Press II,27; the Viking Press III,27; Yale University Press I,20, I,30, II,2, II,15.

INTRODUCTION

(i) *Elizabethan People*

Order and hierarchy dominate much of the thought of Elizabethan England. They were applied equally to the structure of the universe as to the structure of society. And all this was taken to be a reflection of the divine order with God at its apex and the various degrees of angels, men, animals, and inanimate objects below. These theories were all the more emphasised in an age of rising population and social dislocation.

We tend to think of the Queen, the apex of this pyramid, as Gloriana, the incarnation of her age, immortalised in God-like splendour by the portrait painters of her later years. We must not, however, allow these idealised pictures of the Queen's old age to mask the woman beneath the splendour. Elizabeth's striking personality changed and developed during her reign of forty-five years—the talented girl in her early twenties (I. 1) was clearly very different from the irascible and frequently embittered old woman of the 1590s (I. 5, 6). The Queen did, however, retain certain characteristics throughout her life, notable among them a love of music and splendid clothes (I. 2, 4) and a belief in the necessity of a magnificent Court (I. 3) which paid tribute both to her own dignity and to the majesty of England. During her reign the traditional gulf between the monarch and even the mightiest of subjects was made to seem still wider than usual because Elizabeth had no close relations.

Under the Queen, English society can conveniently be considered, following William Harrison (I. 7), in four classes: gentlemen, citizens and burgesses, yeomen, and the 'fourth sort', the remainder of the population. The most fundamental distinction, a political as well as a social one, was between the gentlemen and the rest. The gentlemen of England, enshrined for ever in Sir Thomas Smith's famous definition (I. 10), comprised—prominent burgesses excepted—the Elizabethan 'political nation', those who took an active part or interest in English government at either central or local level.

Foremost among those of gentle rank were the titled nobility. The peerage under Elizabeth remained a very small group, fifty-seven at the beginning of the reign, fifty-five at the end. Their birth as such gave them no automatic claim to be appointed to the highest government offices—though many peers did become Privy Councillors and high officials—but their social prestige, firmly supported by the Queen and founded on a combination of birth and wealth, was unchallenged. It is true that the peerage as a class probably passed through a temporary financial crisis at the very end of the reign, and throughout the Elizabethan period there were some relatively poor peers and a few who ruined themselves by their extravagance (I. 8); but these facts cannot conceal the truism that the nobility included in its ranks many of the very wealthiest individuals in the country.

Below the peerage in the social hierarchy came the gentry—knights, esquires, and simple gentlemen (I. 10). There were probably about 550 knights at the end of the reign, as many as a quarter of whom had been created by the Earl of Essex during his military and naval campaigns in Ireland and Europe; and there were many thousands of esquires and gentlemen (I. 11). They filled the posts in local and central government from the office of justice of the peace upwards, and like their social superiors in the peerage enjoyed a standard of living which was commensurate with their status in society (I. 9, 12, 13).

The second social class distinguished by Harrison, citizens and burgesses, were of less political importance. Elizabethan England was overwhelmingly rural. With the exception of London no English town had as many as 20,000 inhabitants. The largest, Norwich, Bristol, and a few others, had wealthy merchants among their burgesses, but only the leading citizens of London had resources which put them on a par with wealthier members of the peerage (I. 15). The richest of all London merchants of this period, Sir John Spencer, was probably worth over £300,000 when he died in 1610, almost certainly the richest man in England. Most citizens, of course, were in a very different category from these great urban princes, though many of them reached a modest prosperity.

Harrison's third group, the yeomen, most but not all of them freeholders, probably comprised at least 100,000 families (I. 14, 16). The fourth category of the population included the great bulk of the Queen's subjects, from respectable tradesmen and husbandmen to paupers (I. 17). During good times the more prosperous members of this unprivileged mass of the people lived reasonably well, but even they seldom had any reserves to fall back on in times of trouble, and the great and growing number of paupers had no possessions at all (I. 18, 19). Their lot was always a hard one, and it was worst of all if they found themselves in prison (I. 28).

Famine, plague and war were the three great scourges of early modern European society and Elizabethan England had to endure all three. There were frequent outbreaks of plague throughout the reign, with specially severe epidemics in London in 1563 and 1593 (I. 30); and although in the years following the Queen's accession, up to and including the 1580s, harvests were on the whole good, there was a very bad run in the mid 1590s (I. 31). The severe distress which these brought was aggravated by the fact that they coincided with years of war. England was engaged in a war of attrition in Ireland, and was also at war with Spain from 1585 until the end of the reign; and the struggle led not only to increased taxation but helped to produce social dislocation made worse by price inflation. In such circumstances it is not surprising that discharged soldiers and sailors—some of them starving— were involved in disorders (I. 29), particularly noticeable during the famine years of the mid 1590s.

Although the Spanish war had a disruptive effect on English society, it was at first popular. This was partly because Spain was regarded by most Protestant Englishmen as the main temporal ally of Antichrist, as personified by the Pope, but partly also because of a general chauvinism which was one of the most notable characteristics of the English people in Elizabeth's reign (I. 21, 22, 24). That chauvinism was very noticeable in London, where a rapidly expanding population, engaged in a great variety of trades (I. 25 and II. 15), was crowded closely together. Foreigners walking in London streets, which were thronged by an ever growing number of coaches (I. 26) and crowded with elegantly dressed women, might well be pushed out of the way by apprentices, who were only too ready to resort to other and more serious forms of violence in an age when minor quarrels could rapidly develop into full-scale riots (I. 23, 24, 27).

This violent, hierarchically organised society spoke a vigorous language which grew increasingly rich and flexible in the second half of the sixteenth century to find its fullest expression in the greatest age of poetry and drama which England has ever known (I. 35).

(ii) *The Economy*

At a time when England's political survival was at risk, much depended on her economic resources. A gloomy commentator at the beginning of the reign saw the position as well-nigh desperate (II. 1). The Queen inherited a critical inflationary situation, which previous efforts had failed to solve; but a vigorous re-coinage policy considerably improved the position (II. 2). Yet the inflation had deeper roots than the debased currency and was derived, in large measure, from the growth of population, at a faster pace than any possible expansion in the means to feed or employ them. Hence, too many people were chasing too few goods and too few jobs and, as usually happens in these circumstances, prices rose and wages fell. Lambarde (II. 3) and others comment on the growth of population but not on the direct link between it and inflation. What statesmen and pamphleteers were aware of, and alarmed by, was social instability, especially the movement from the land, through eviction or in men's search for jobs. The statutes and other records are full of arguments and policies to maintain a stable rural population (II. 4, 5).

But the upheaval taking place in the lives of the peasantry formed part of a continuing change in the whole structure of rural society. Contemporaries were very conscious of the social mobility of their time, that the nobility, gentry, yeomanry, merchants, industrialists were not permanently bound to their station in society: some made fortunes and rose high, others lost fortunes and declined. And apart from dramatic changes, social relations were relatively fluid, more fluid than anxious statesmen cared to contemplate. But what contemporaries could not agree about was which group was suffering the most, which gaining the most, from these changes (II. 6, 7). It is as yet impossible to assess the degree of depopulation that was taking place: it varied enormously from district to district. Even if the amount was exaggerated, a small change could greatly add to the sense of insecurity (II. 8). As against this, however, there is plenty of evidence of voluntary enclosure, that is, the re-distribution of land by agreement (II. 9). The other threat to order came from food shortage, at a time when agrarian improvement could not be carried through to a sufficient extent to meet growing needs (II. 11, 12), though in times of plenty some regions had a surplus for export (II. 10).

In industry, also, significant changes were taking place, though the effects were not extensively felt until later. The only major English industry was the production of unfinished woollen textiles, itself undergoing change as the result of market developments, especially at Antwerp. Attempts were made to encourage the finishing industry in England (II. 16), but with not much success in the Elizabethan period. We notice, however, the increasing diversification of industry in the provinces; and in London, in particular, a variety of trades flourished as was to be expected in a growing capital city (II. 15). But there were also renewed attempts to control industrial production by parliament, local authorities, and the great industrial and commercial companies

(II. 13, 14). To relieve unemployment town authorities were sometimes required to keep stocks to set the poor to work (II. 17); but these measures were of limited value since industrial unemployment resulting from a slump in demand was not curable by piling up further local stocks.

We notice during the period developments in heavy industry, including coal (II. 18, 19), the promise rather than the achievement of major industrial advance. But to encourage capital and skill to come forward to develop and finance new industries, patents of monopoly were granted to groups of investors (II. 19), as indeed they are granted today; in the late sixteenth century, however, they were often given to control various industries and trades, not as necessary protective measures but as privileges to investors, with a consequent outcry in parliament and elsewhere (II. 20).

Trade, both in imports and exports, was like industry diversifying (II. 21) and, at the same time, there was a bitter controversy over whether trade should be free, i.e. not free from tariffs but free for private traders, or whether a massive company, the Merchant Adventurers, should control the greater part of overseas trade (II. 22, 23, 24). There was meanwhile the renewal of an old controversy over the taking of interest. The medieval prohibitions of interest on religious grounds gave birth to all sorts of disguised and contorted instruments for borrowing money and paying interest. But, if investment was to be encouraged it must be sure that the taking of interest was legalised. This was done in 1545, it was once again prohibited in 1552, and again lawfully established in 1571 (II. 25); but long afterwards the traditional hostility to it remained (II. 26). The legalisation of interest was one indication of the growing sophistication of industry and trade; another was the relatively advanced technique of commercial insurance (II. 27).

(iii) *Intellectual developments*

The English Renaissance was slow in coming; and it was not until well into the Elizabethan period that we see many signs of a secular, diversified culture as well as the impact of recent scientific thought. Yet even so the traditional outlook remained the most powerful influence. For example, Burghley's advice to his son, Thomas, is cast in a conservative mould with especial emphasis on the established faith (III. 1, see also V. 13). The severe outlook of the statesman is matched by the austere conditions of school life, though liberal educationalists like Roger Ascham were arguing for a more humane approach to the whole question (III. 2, 3). This coincided with an increasing awareness of the need for more schools; and the endowment of educational institutions by laymen was a marked feature of Elizabethan England (III. 4). At the same time men like Richard Mulcaster were advocating reforms so that the traditionally dominant role of the classics could be reduced (III. 5).

Educational expansion was a notable feature also of the two (and only) universities, at Oxford and Cambridge (III. 6), while the Inns of Court in London were conceived of by contemporaries as the third university (III. 7). According to some, expansion had not been accompanied by a maintenance of standards while Thomas Hobbes, looking back at these developments, saw the universities as the breeding ground for radical extremists (III. 8, 9).

As the Church increasingly lost some, but not all, its hold over education as well as the arts, the role of the lay patron grew in importance. The Earl of Leicester was one of many courtiers whose support was much sought after; and we have evidence that he took his duties very seriously, rendering especial help to Puritan scholars (III. 10, 12). The Earl of Bedford was even more closely identified with the patronage of Puritans (III. 11). But patronage had its counter-part in faction; and able men like Spenser and Bacon, who found themselves on the losing side, might find that their talents were inadequately used and rewarded (III. 13). Bacon, indeed, whose essay 'Of Studies' is as fresh as on the day it was written (III. 15), questioned the relevance of patronage in the world of literature (III. 14) though he would hardly have expected that it could be eliminated in politics.

By the second half of the sixteenth century governments all over Europe were aware that the printing press could, in the matter of politics or religion, serve conflicting purposes. It could be used in defence of the existing order, as it was by Tudor governments in proclamations, homilies, pamphlets and other ways; but it could also be employed to disseminate minority—sometimes hostile—opinion. Hence the growth of official censorship (III. 16, 17) as well as the punishment of pamphleteers like John Stubbes (V. 2). But, in spite of various restraints, the late Elizabethan period witnessed unparalleled achievements in English literature. Historical works by men like Camden (III. 18) and Stow (III. 19) indicate some aspects of the movement away from chronicle and legend, which had begun earlier in the century, and they displayed serious attempts to use critically the available records, though some tart observations by Sir Philip Sidney draw attention to certain of the prejudices and vanities of historians of his age—and our own (III. 20).

The Court now held a central place in all branches of the arts and entertainment (III. 21). But it was in drama that both Court and capital, as well as some of the private companies of leading courtiers, made so great a contribution. Middleton comments on the conflicting aims of playwrights in a manner which reflects some of the tensions of our modern theatre (III. 22); and in a famous passage his contemporary, Shakespeare, has some frank advice to give to the actors of his day (III. 23). But the Puritan hostility to the theatre in the later part of the Elizabethan period directed the attack on the moral laxity of play-wright, actors, and audience (III. 24) and foreshadowed the shutting down of the theatres in 1642. The poets came closest to the dramatists in the brilliance of their work; and the life of Sidney in its genius and tragedy symbolised certain aspects of the gilded aristocracy of his generation (III. 25). It is worth recording, however, that poetry was not the preserve of cultivated aristocrats; and we have used a ballad, of no intrinsic merit, to illustrate the vast production of contemporary verse, much of it patriotic (III. 26).

In science, the discoveries in astronomy received in Elizabethan England a mixed reception, ranging from the skilful defence of Copernicus by Digges (III. 27) to scornful rejection by Blundevile (III. 28). In pharmacy and medicine progress was also made, though much of it was hit or miss. Our documents illustrate some of the early illusions held about tobacco (III. 29) as well as the survival of ancient—and dangerous—remedies in medicine (III. 30). Bacon puts his finger on some of the weaknesses in medical education and practice (III. 31). What is clear, however, is that new intellectual approaches in the arts and sciences were undermining the faith in a stable order in the universe as well as in religion, politics and society. Donne reveals the deep sense of uncertainty which preceded some of the great changes of the seventeenth century (III. 32).

(iv) Religion

The Elizabethan religious settlement of 1559, as set out in the acts of Supremacy and Uniformity (IV. 1, 2), was a compromise between the views of a conservative queen and a more radical House of Commons. It created a royal supremacy over the Church which was indubitably parliamentary and thus very different from the supremacy of Eliza-beth's father, Henry VIII, which was recognised by parliament but not based on its authority (IV. 4).

The traditional administrative structure of the Church, with its archbishops, bishops and archdeacons, continued under this settlement

(IV. 3), and these dignitaries were all subject to the new High Commission which exercised the Queen's ecclesiastical prerogative but was also authorised by the Act of Supremacy (IV. 1, 5). Elizabeth's own attitude towards the Church was compounded of a mixture of faith, determination, resignation and cynicism. Despite parliament's authorisation of the royal supremacy in 1559 she was determined, throughout her reign, to prevent the House of Commons from interfering in ecclesiastical affairs. At the same time she was resigned to the inevitability of some corruption in church administration (IV. 8), and she cynically plundered the Church's wealth on the authority of a statute of 1559 which enabled her, during her reign, to seize many of the most desirable episcopal estates, which she then frequently leased on favourable terms to her courtiers. This was formally done by an 'exchange' always unfavourable to the Church (IV. 10). In her eyes the Church as an institution was essentially part of the state and its administration; and, although she had certain ingrained prejudices—she would, for example, have preferred a celibate clergy (IV. 11)—she was entirely free from the kind of religious enthusiasm which inspired many of the best minds of the age. With those ideas, she quite naturally regarded bishops as primarily servants of the royal will, and when Archbishop Grindal refused, on grounds of conscience, to obey her orders, he was promptly suspended from the exercise of his jurisdiction (IV. 9, 15).

This kind of interference in ecclesiastical affairs by a temporal sovereign—and worst of all by one who was also a woman—was one of the aspects of the Church of England which was quite unacceptable to Catholics. Indeed, almost from the beginning of the reign, the Church was under fire from both Catholics and Puritans; both saw it as merely a human creation, the Catholics denying that it had any basis in Christian tradition, the Puritans denying that its structure had any scriptural authority. This challenge was met by two notable churchmen, John Jewel, Bishop of Salisbury, and the 'judicious' Richard Hooker, who produced philosophical justifications of the Church (IV. 12, 13). By representing it as a return to the true forms of early Christianity, free from the excesses of both Popery and Puritanism, they made it intellectually respectable.

Puritanism and Catholicism were of course serious threats to the Elizabethan Church. The word Puritan began to be used in the 1560s to describe men who wished to 'purify' the Church by stripping it of its Catholic relics. Of course, they differed among themselves as to what was intolerable. The earliest Puritans were mostly moderates who accepted episcopal government of the Church but took a stand against the hierarchy's attempts in the 1560s to enforce the use of the surplice in church services—no attempt was made by the bishops to insist on the use of the medieval mass vestments which had been authorised by the Act of Uniformity (IV. 2). The unpopularity which many bishops drew upon themselves because of their role in this vestiarian controversy led to a more extreme phase in the Puritan movement, which was characterised by attacks on the institution of episcopacy itself. This assault was led by Thomas Cartwright who, while he was Lady Margaret Professor of Divinity at Cambridge in 1569–70, had given a course of lectures which advocated a presbyterian type of organisation for the Church. This proposed polity is set out in the *Second Admonition to Parliament* of 1572, which was probably written by Cartwright himself (IV. 14). The agitation greatly alarmed the Queen, and she was constantly on the watch for anything which might smack of Presbyterianism, which was, as she rightly observed in a later address to parliament, 'dangerous to a kingly rule' (IV. 8). It was such fears which led her to suppress the 'prophesyings' which had grown up in various parts of England during the 1560s and 1570s. These were local meetings of the clergy and laity for prayer, instruction and personal improvement, and the Queen's decision provoked a courageous and justly famous letter from Grindal (IV. 15), which led to his suspension from 1577 until his death in 1583. His successor, the fiercely anti-Puritan Whitgift, inaugurated a campaign to remove nonconformists from their benefices by requiring subscription to three articles (IV. 16), one at least of which was unacceptable to even the more moderate Puritans. Opposition at Court and in the Privy Council forced him to compromise, at least to the extent of allowing qualified subscription, and few Puritans seem to have been deprived; but at the end of the 1580s and during the early 1590s, when the Puritan movement had been weakened by the death of its greatest patron, the Earl of Leicester (IV. 19), and by the obloquy which the vituperative Marprelate tracts brought upon the movement as a whole, Whitgift was able to use Star Chamber and the High Commission to crush the organised Presbyterian movement which had grown to considerable strength in the Church by the 1580s. It went underground and only reappeared to a limited extent in the summer of 1603, when James I's decision to hold the Hampton Court Conference seemed to presage more favourable treatment for the Puritans.

One of the most striking characteristics of the Puritan movement was its emphasis on preaching, and most of the able preachers of the age, like Henry Smith (IV. 18), had Puritan leanings. Puritanism also produced notable piety among many, but by no means all, of its lay adherents, not least in the 1590s, when, despite the disappearance of organised Presbyterianism, a more moderate Puritanism, which stressed the virtues of Sabbatarianism and of religious observances centred on the household (IV. 17), continued to be very strong among the laity.

It is tempting to distinguish clearly between Puritanism and Anglicanism in the Elizabethan period, but this, as Professor Dickens reminds us, is anachronistic. Puritanism was a tendency within the Church of England—there were very few separatists in Elizabeth's reign—and the position of a man like archbishop Grindal, a primate who was dismissed for refusing to suppress 'Puritan' exercises, reminds us of the complexities of the situation.

The involved relationship between Puritanism and the Church of England cannot, of course, be paralleled by any similar links between the Church of England and Catholicism. The Queen hoped that Catholics, deprived of firm direction from abroad in the early years of the reign, would be starved of clerical instruction and encouragement as the Catholic priests who still managed to perform their functions in the 1560s grew old and died. The issue of the Papal Bull of deposition against the Queen in 1570 (IV. 20) and the increasing influx of secular priests from abroad from 1574 onwards, and of Jesuits from 1580, rendered such hopes illusory. The new priests, though trained abroad, were Englishmen, devoted to sustaining the faith of those fellow countrymen who had remained true to the old religion and determined to convert or reconvert others. But their subjection to the jurisdiction of a foreign prince—the Pope—made it possible for the English government to pass laws of increasing severity against them and their fellow Catholics from 1571 onwards, culminating in the penalties of treason. As a result, over 180 Catholics were executed during the later years of the reign. Many of them, like the Jesuit Edmund Campion, welcomed martyrdom (IV. 23). William Cecil's statement that these men died as traitors (IV. 21) had some plausibility, but so too had the claim of the Catholic apologist, William Allen, later a cardinal, that they died for the sake of religion (IV. 22). The historian should probably conclude that both Cecil and Allen were, in a sense, right in an age when religion and politics were so closely intertwined.

Few Englishmen, of course, even approached the religious fervour of Catholic and Puritan enthusiasts and it is probable that most people were merely formally devout, attending church services—at which they often behaved with scant decency (IV. 24)—as a social duty which was required and enforced by the state. On the other hand, almost all of them had conventional beliefs in God and in the fundamentals of the

Christian faith. Few can have been as genuinely sceptical as Sir Walter Raleigh (IV. 25), although even he was almost certainly not an atheist.

(v) Government and Administration

Elizabeth fully accepted the idea that she was God's minister (V. 1), and had the very highest conception of her rights. For her the royal prerogative was inviolable and she defended it jealously throughout her reign. Her most trusted ministers were only asked for advice when she thought fit (V. 4), she accepted or rejected their counsel at her own discretion (V. 3, 5), and any private subject, such as the luckless John Stubbes, who trespassed on her exclusive authority in affairs of state was liable to pay a heavy penalty for his presumption (V. 2).

One of the most important elements in the Queen's success in government was her policy of 'divide and rule' (V. 6). William Cecil, created Lord Burghley in 1571, was her most influential adviser throughout her reign (V. 10), but he never monopolised her confidence; and in the period up to 1588 she used the personal rivalry and political differences which existed between Burghley and Robert Dudley, Earl of Leicester, to retain her own independence and ensure that the Privy Council, which was divided between their supporters (V. 9), remained her servant and did not threaten to become her master. She probably hoped to maintain this kind of balance in the 1590s, with Burghley's role being filled by his younger son Robert Cecil, whom he had trained in his own image (V. 13), and Leicester's by his stepson and political heir Robert Devereux, the brilliant but unstable Earl of Essex. This plan, if it really existed in the Queen's mind, was quite unworkable. Essex totally lacked the moderation which would have been necessary to ensure its success (V. 11). He wanted to dominate both Court and Council completely, and when the Queen refused high political office to himself and his friends he first of all sulked and then tried vainly to recoup his reputation in Ireland. His failure there and subsequent revolt and execution meant the end of the classic Elizabethan political system. Essex's fall left Robert Cecil virtually supreme.

All the prominent politicians in the Elizabethan period were members of the Privy Council and we have seen that the Council was divided by faction throughout the reign. The conflicts among the councillors, which reflected both personal rivalries and political differences, must not be allowed to conceal the fact that most of the Council's work was routine and largely non-controversial. As the chief administrative authority in the realm it controlled the governmental machinery of the country, concerned with everything which went on in England. It was also subjected to the pleas of private suitors, who sought its judicial authority to settle cases which should often have been brought before the ordinary courts. During the later years of the reign the war with Spain and the increasing complexities of its public domestic duties—especially those connected with overseeing the growing work of the justices of the peace—led to a great increase in its work and to attempts to restrict the access of private citizens to it (V. 7). These efforts did not succeed, however, and at the end of the reign the Council was heavily overburdened with routine business.

The Privy Council was strong. How strong was parliament? This has been the subject of debate from Elizabethan times on to our own. In the Queen's view it remained essentially a body to pass legislation, grant taxation and comment helpfully on matters set before it. Sir Thomas Smith, though he gives it greater importance than that and considers it a body which represents the whole nation, gives no indication of how far Members of the House of Commons had the right to speak freely or introduce bills concerning religious, diplomatic or other matters (V. 14). The redoubtable Peter Wentworth, however, claimed rights which went well beyond the established view, with unfortunate consequences for himself (V. 15). The Queen's affirmation of her authority in parliament, given through the Lord Keeper, set severe limits to Members' rights (V. 16); and on the whole she kept a firm grip on the institution. But in the event Wentworth indicated the shape of things to come in the next century. One of the most influential figures in applying policy generally, and guiding the House of Commons, was the Secretary of State (V. 17); but the strength of the office depended on the standing and skill of the holder.

Yet success in government depended upon adequate funds to govern; and the sources indicate the difficulties in this sphere which confronted the Queen at the beginning of the reign (V. 18), and which became severe in the war years at the end (V. 19, 20). Success depended also upon the strength of the law courts to see that justice would be done and be seen to be done. But the powers of the common law courts, such as King's Bench or the Assizes (V. 21, 25), were limited by the rigidity of some of their methods as well as by the weaknesses inherent in a jury system. As against these the prerogative courts, especially Star Chamber, offered swift and firm justice (V. 22); but when it came to treason the common law courts or special commissions could display notable speed and power (V. 23).

In the shires themselves, however, much depended on the justices of the peace, at quarter sessions, or sometimes acting as individuals or in groups, to uphold the law and administer the shire (V. 24, 25, 26). One of the striking features of Elizabethan local government was the vast increase of duties imposed on J.P.s; and, where their interests did not conflict with government policy, they could be invaluable instruments of the central power. But they were amateurs and part-time, virtually unpaid, servants of the crown. The Queen had many other part-time and full-time servants and these men received some or all of their remuneration from gifts from suitors for services rendered (V. 27). In the existing system, with a government inadequately supplied with revenue to maintain a Civil Service, private payments were not necessarily corrupt, though they could easily give rise to corruption. This inherent poverty in the Elizabethan system of government was visible in all its branches right up to the Court itself (V. 28). The other basic weakness lay in political patronage which, though inherent and essential, could have shattering consequences on the careers of those in the wrong faction. In the famous poem, *The Lie*, we have the most bitter indictment of a governmental order on the eve of its decline (V. 29).

I

ELIZABETHAN PEOPLE

1 The heiress to the throne: Princess Elizabeth at the age of twenty-three

This account of Elizabeth some eighteen months before she came to the throne was written in May 1557 by Giovanni Michiel, Venetian ambassador to the Court of Queen Mary, in the course of a long report to the Doge and Senate about conditions in England. It shows the great impression which her intellectual abilities and political skill could make, even in her early twenties, on foreign observers. It is worth noting the attention which Michiel draws to Elizabeth's fine hands, which remained perhaps her most beautiful and striking feature to the end of her life.

She is a young woman whose mind is considered no less excellent than her person, although her face is comely rather than handsome, but she is tall and well formed, with a good skin . . . ; she has fine eyes and above all a beautiful hand of which she makes a display; and her intellect and understanding are wonderful, as she showed very plainly by her conduct when in danger and under suspicion. As a linguist she excels the Queen, for besides Latin she has no slight knowledge of Greek, and speaks Italian more than the Queen does, taking so much pleasure in it that from vanity she will never speak any other language with Italians.

Cal. S.P. Venetian, vi, part ii (1556–7),
pp. 1058–9

2 A royal musician

In the autumn of 1564 Sir James Melville, a sophisticated courtier, visited England as the representative of Mary, Queen of Scots. He found Elizabeth very curious about his mistress and in the course of discussion she asked about Mary's abilities as a musician. Melville replied that his mistress played 'reasonably' well on the lute and on the virginals—the latter a keyed musical instrument much favoured at the time. Elizabeth, who had a considerable interest in music and was an accomplished performer on both virginals and lute, later demonstrated her own skill to Melville. Her surprise at seeing the envoy need not be accepted at its face value. The incident was probably planned in advance. Nor can Melville's Memoirs, written long after the event, be wholly trusted.

My Lord of Hunsdon drew me up to a quiet gallery . . . where I might hear the Queen play upon the virginals. . . . After I had hearkened awhile, I took by the tapestry that hung before the door of the chamber and, seeing her back was toward the door, I entered within the chamber . . . , and heard her play excellently well; but she left off as soon as she turned her about and saw me, and came forward, seeming to strike me with her left hand . . . , alleging that she used not to play before men, but when she was solitary . . . , to eschew melancholy.'

James Melville, *Memoirs* (Edinburgh, 1827), p. 124

3 The Queen in public

Lupold von Wedel, a German nobleman and an enthusiastic traveller who visited much of Europe and the Middle East during the course of his life, left a most interesting description of England in the 1580s, including an account of the Queen at Hampton Court, the great palace built by Cardinal Wolsey, which quickly passed into the hands of Henry VIII and remained one of the more notable royal residences during the Tudor period. Von Wedel's account gives us a fascinating glimpse of Elizabeth in public. Although she herself was dressed in mourning for William of Orange who had been murdered in June 1584 and for her former suitor the Duke of Alençon, who had died in the same month, the Court paraded in all its accustomed splendour. The scene goes far to justify foreigners' virtually unanimous opinion that the English Court was one of the most splendid in Europe.

On the 18th [October 1584] we walked a mile between walls which surrounded two gardens and which reach as far as Hampton Court, where the Queen resides. As it was Sunday we went to the church or chapel which is in the palace. This chapel is well decorated with a beautiful organ, silver gilt, with large and small silver pipes. Before the Queen marched her lifeguard, all chosen men, strong and tall, two hundred in number, we were told, though not all of them were present. They bore gilt halberts, red coats faced with black velvet in front and on the back they wore the Queen's arms silver gilt. Then came gentlemen of rank and of the council, two of them bearing a royal sceptre

each, a third with the royal sword in a red velvet scabbard, embroidered
with gold and set with precious stones and large pearls. Now came the
Queen, dressed in black on account of the death of the Prince of Orange
and the Duke of Alençon; on each side of her curly hair she wore a
large pearl of the size of a hazelnut. The people standing on both sides
fell on their knees, but she showed herself very gracious, and accepted
with an humble mien letters of supplication from rich and poor. Her
train was carried behind her by a countess, then followed twelve young
ladies of noble birth, children of counts or lords. . . . Both sides of the
gallery as far as the Queen walked through it to the chapel were lined
by the guard bearing arms. As the day was almost gone there was no
sermon, only singing and delivering prayers. Then the Queen returned
as she had come and went to her room, and when on her passing the
people fell on their knees, she said in English: 'Thank you with all my
heart.' Now eight trumpeters clad in red gave the signal for dinner, and
did it very well. Afterwards two drummers and a piper made music
according to the English fashion, and we betook ourselves to our
lodgings.

'Journey through England and Scotland made
by Lupold von Wedel in the years 1584 and
1585', *TRHS*, New Series, ix (1895), pp.
250–51

4   An unwelcome sermon

Sir John Harington, Elizabeth's godson, left some of the best descriptions
which we possess of her in her later years. This episode comes from the 1590s—
we do not know the exact date—and the bishop may have been John Aylmer,
who occupied the see of London between 1577 and 1594. It is easy to understand the Queen's sensitivity about her wardrobe. She left many hundreds of
dresses, and even in the 1590s, a time of war, social distress and financial strin-
gency, she was able to find large sums of money to purchase jewels for her own
adornment. It may seem a selfish, unattractive aspect of her complex character,
but it was a characteristic feature of Renaissance monarchy, which regarded
display as an aspect of power.

One Sunday . . . my Lord of London preached to the Queen's Majesty
and seemed to touch on the vanity of decking the body too finely. Her
Majesty told the ladies that 'if the bishop held more discourse on such
matters, she would fit him for Heaven—but he should walk thither
without a staff and leave his mantle behind him'. Perchance the bishop

8 The wealth of the peerage

Thomas Wilson, the younger son of a country gentleman, had a versatile career in the law, politics, business and the academic world in the Elizabethan and Jacobean periods, but did not achieve conspicuous distinction. His main claim to fame lies in his authorship of 'The State of England, *anno. dom.* 1600', which contains as its most remarkable feature an estimate of the numbers and incomes of the different sections of the upper classes in the community. This passage gives his estimate of the total revenue of the nobility at the end of the Elizabethan period as £220,000 *per annum*, a figure which may not be very wide of the mark in view of Professor Stone's calculation that the peerage in 1602 had a total gross income of £195,000 *per annum*.

I have seen divers books which have been collected by secretaries and counsellors of estate which did exactly show the several revenues of every nobleman, knights and gentlemen through the realm. . . . But it were too long in this simple discourse to set down the particularities thereof. But conferring these books together I find great alterations almost every year, so mutable are wordly things and worldly men's affairs; as namely the earl of Oxford, who in the year 1575 was rated at £12,000 a year sterling, within 2 following was vanished and no name of him found, having in that time prodigally spent and consumed all, even to the selling of the stones, timber and lead of his castles and houses. And yet he liveth and hath the first place amongst earls, but the Queen is his gracious mistress and gives him maintenance for his nobility sake, but (to say the truth) out of the bishopric of Ely, which since his decay could never see other bishop. And other, the earl of Arundel about the same time was reckoned not much inferior to him in state and before him in dignity, and in one 6 months all was confiscate to the Queen for treason. The other earls some daily decay, some increase according to the course of the world, but that which I have noted by perusing many of the said books, and of the later sort, is that still the total sum groweth much to one reckoning, and that is to £100,000 rent yearly, accounting them all in gross to avoid prolixity. If a man would proportion this amongst 19 earls and a marquis it would be no great matter, to every one £5,000 rent, but as some exceed that much, so many come short of it.

The 39 barons and 2 viscounts do not much exceed that sum; their revenue is reckoned together to amount to £120,000 yearly.

T. Wilson, 'The State of England, *anno. dom.* 1600', *Camden Misc.*, ed. F. J. Fisher, xvi (1936), pp. 21–2

9   The nobility at table

The nobility of England—or at least the great majority of them—were devoted to the idea of conspicuous consumption. In the Elizabethan period they spent vast sums on buildings, on clothes, and on their funerals and tombs. In an age which laid stress on the duties of hospitality, especially among the great, they also provided lavish supplies of food for themselves and their guests, as the following excerpt from Harrison makes clear.

In number of dishes and change of meat the nobility of England (whose cooks are for the most part musical-headed Frenchmen and strangers) do most exceed, since there is no day . . . that passeth over their heads, wherein they have not only beef, mutton, veal, lamb, kid, pork, cony, capon, pig, or so many of these as the season yieldeth, but also some portion of the red or fallow deer, beside great variety of fish and wild fowl, and thereto sundry other delicates wherein the sweet hand of the seafaring Portingale [i.e. Portuguese] is not wanting: so that for a man to dine with one of them, and to taste of every dish that standeth before him, which few use to do . . . , is rather to yield unto a conspiracy with a great deal of meat for the speedy suppression of natural health than the use of a necessary mean to satisfy himself with a competent repast to sustain his body withal.

W. Harrison, Description of England, ed.
F. J. Furnivall (1877), i, 144–5

10   The gentry

The titular nobility made up the upper ranks of English society. Below them came knights, esquires and simple gentlemen. This passage, which deals with these non-noble gentlemen or gentry, was written during the 1560s by Sir Thomas Smith who was, during the course of his career, Secretary of State to both King Edward VI and Queen Elizabeth. It comes from his *De Republica Anglorum*, the only satisfactory contemporary treatise on the English constitution, and contains his famous definition of a gentleman—undoubtedly the classic Elizabethan description. The coat of arms, which was obtained from the College of Heralds, was the formal acknowledgement of gentility.

No man is a knight by succession, not the king or prince. . . . Knights, therefore, be not born but made, either before the battle to encourage them the more to adventure their lives, or after the conflict, as advancement for their hardiness and manhood already showed: or out of the war for some great service done, or some good hope through the virtues which do appear in them. And they are made either by the king himself . . . , or by his lieutenant in the wars, who hath his royal and absolute power committed to him for that time. . . .

Esquire[s] . . . be all those which bear arms . . . which to bear is a testimony of the nobility or race from whence they do come. These be taken for no distinct order of the common wealth, but do go with the residue of the gentlemen: save that (as I take it) they be those who bear arms, testimonies (as I have said) of their race, and therefore have neither creation nor dubbing. . . .

As for gentlemen, they be made good cheap in England. For whosoever studieth the laws of the realm, who studieth in the universities, who professeth liberal sciences, and to be short, who can live idly and without manual labour and will bear the port, charge and countenance of a gentleman, he shall be called master, for that is the title which men give to esquires and other gentlemen, and shall be taken for a gentleman. . . . And if need be a king of heralds shall also give him for money arms newly made and invented, the title whereof shall pretend to have been found by the said herald in perusing and viewing of old registers, where his ancestors in times past had been recorded to bear the same. Or if he will do it more truly and of better faith, he will write that for the merits of that man, and certain qualities which he doth see in him, and for sundry noble acts which he hath performed, he by the authority which he hath as king of heralds and arms, giveth to him and his heirs these and these arms, which being done I think he may be called a[n] [e]squire, for he beareth ever after those arms. . . .

Thomas Smith, *De Republica Anglorum*, ed.
L. Alston (Cambridge, 1906), pp. 32–40

11 Prosperous gentlemen and wealthy lawyers

Thomas Wilson's estimate of the numbers and revenues of the different sections of the gentry and of the wealth of the lawyers—who would, of course, have been included by contemporaries among the 'gentlemen'—is unique. His estimate of 500 knights in 1600, excluding the notorious creations of the Earl of Essex, though probably rather high, may not be very wide of the mark, but it is impossible, in the present state of historical research, to judge the validity of his other figures. Nevertheless, in view of the flood of contemporary comment upon the wealth and numbers of the common lawyers, his picture of their great prosperity, in what was a notoriously litigious age, may be accepted in general terms.

There are accounted to be in England about the number of 500 knights
as I have reckoned them. . . . I reckon not among them my lord of
Essex knights . . . , but such as are chief men in their counties both for
living and reputations. . . . These for the most part are men for living
betwixt £1,000 and £2,000 yearly, and many of them equal the best
barons and come not much behind many earls . . . viz. Sir John Petre,
Sir John Harington, Sir Nicholas Bacon and others, who are thought to
be able to dispend yearly betwixt £5,000 and £7,000 of good land.

Those which we call esquires are gentlemen whose ancestors are or
have been knights, or else they are the heirs and eldest of their houses
and of some competent quantity of revenue fit to be called to office and
authority in their country where they live. Of these there are esteemed
to be in England, as I have seen by the book of musters of every several
shire, to the number of 16,000 or thereabout, whereof there are of
[them] in commissions of the peace about 1,400 in every province—in
some 40, in some 50, some 30, more or less. These are men in living
betwixt £1,000 and £500 rent. Especially about London and the
counties adjoining, where their lands are set to the highest, he is not
counted of any great reckoning unless he be betwixt 1,000 marks or
£1,000, but northward and far off a gentleman of good reputation may
be content with £300 and £400 yearly. These are the elder brothers.

I cannot speak of the [number] of younger brothers, albeit I be one of
the number myself, but for their estate there is no man hath better
cause to know it, nor less cause to praise it.

[The common lawyers] . . . within these 40 or 50 years, since the
practice of civil law hath been as it were wholly banished and abrogated, and since the clergy hath been trodden down by the taking away
of church livings, and since the long continuance of peace hath bred an
inward canker and rest in men's minds, the people doing nothing but
jar and wrangle one with another, these lawyers by the ruins of
neighbours' contentions, are grown so great, so rich and so proud that
no other sort dare meddle with them. Their number is so great now
that, to say the truth, they can scarcely live one by another, the practice
being drawn into a few hand of those which are most renowned, and
all the rest live by pettifogging, seeking means to set their neighbours
at variance, whereby they may gain on both sides. This is one of the
greatest inconveniences in the land, that the number of the lawyers are
so great they undo the country people and buy up all the lands that are
to be sold, so that young gentlemen or others newly coming to their
livings, some of them prying into his evidence will find the means to
set him at variance with some other, or some other with him, by some

pretence or quiddity, and when they have half consumed themselves in suit, they are fain to sell their land to follow the process and pay their debts, and then that becomes a prey to lawyers.

For the greatness of some of them it is incredible. Not to speak of the 12 chief judges and the multitude of sergeants, which are most of them counted men of £20,000 or £30,000 yearly, there is one at this day of a meaner degree, viz. the Queen's attorney, who, within this 10 years in my knowledge was not able to dispend above £100 a year and now by his own lands, his coins and his office he may dispend betwixt 12 and 14 thousand.

There are in number of sergeants about 30, counsellors about 2,000, and as many attorneys, besides solicitors and pettifoggers an infinite number, there being no province, city, town, nor scarce village free from them, unless the isle of Anglesey, which boast they never had lawyers nor foxes.

> T. Wilson, 'The State of England, *anno dom.*
> 1600', ed. F. J. Fisher, *Camden Misc.*, xvi
> (1936), pp. 23–5

12 The high cost of being a gentleman

The variety and luxury of gentlemen's dress, which is well described in the following passage, caused disapproving comment from many contemporary writers, such as Philip Stubbes and William Harrison, but it must remain an open question whether such extravagance contributed to a decay of traditional hospitality among the gentry. Hospitality, in this context, comprised not only entertainment of one's social equals but distribution of food to the local poor.

. . . I hold this excessive costly apparel a great cause why gentlemen cannot maintain their wonted and accustomed bounty and liberality in hospitality and housekeeping—for, whenas the mercer's book shall come *item* for so many yards of cloth of gold, of silver, velvet, satin, taffeta or suchlike ware; the goldsmith's *debet* for chains, rings, jewels, pearls and precious stones; the tailor's bill, so much for such a suit of laced satin and suchlike superfluous charges, amounting in one year to more than the revenues of his lands.

> I. M. 'A health to the gentlemanly profession
> of servingmen' (1598), in A. Nicoll, *The
> Elizabethans* (Cambridge, 1957), p. 30

13   The pleasures of eating

Whatever the truth of the charge in the last document about the decay of
hospitality among gentlemen, this excerpt from Harrison makes it clear that
when they had guests they fed them well, and that even when they were on
their own they did not by any means starve.

The gentlemen and merchants keep much about one rate, and each of
them contenteth himself with four, five or six dishes when they have
but small resort, or peradventure with one, or two, or three at the most,
when they have no strangers to accompany them at their tables. And
yet their servants have their ordinary diet assigned, beside such as is left
at their masters' boards and not appointed to be brought thither the
second time, which nevertheless is often seen generally in venison,
lamb, or some especial dish, whereon the merchant man himself liketh
to feed when it is cold, or peradventure, for sundry causes incident to
the feeder, is better so, than if it were warm or hot. . . .

W. Harrison, *Description of England*, ed.
F. J. Furnivall (1877), i, 148

14   Burgesses and yeomen

The following definition of citizens and burgesses as the more prosperous
inhabitants of the towns seems unexceptionable, but the idea that the word
yeoman should be confined in a strictly legalistic way to forty shilling freeholders distorts historical reality. Many Elizabethans described as yeomen by
their contemporaries held no freehold land at all, and the best definition would
be to describe the yeoman, in economic terms, as a prosperous farmer, who took
his place in the social scale between the gentleman above and the husbandman
or small farmer below. Modern research confirms that very many yeomen
increased substantially in prosperity during the Elizabethan period. The desire
to send their sons to university and thus make them 'gentlemen' was natural in
the status-conscious society of the time.

Next to gentlemen be appointed citizens and burgesses, such as not
only be free and received as officers within the cities, but also be of
some substance to bear the charges. But these citizens and burgesses be
to serve the common wealth in their cities and boroughs or in corporate
towns where they dwell. . . .
   I call him a yeoman whom our laws do call *legalem hominem*, a word
familiar in writs and inquests, which is a freeman born English and may
dispend of his own free land in yearly revenue to the sum of forty

shillings sterling. . . . This sort of people confess themselves to be no gentlemen, but give the honour to all which be or take upon them to be gentlemen, and yet they have a certain pre-eminence and more estimation than labourers and artificers, and commonly live wealthily, keep good houses, and do their business and travail to acquire riches. These be (for the most part) farmers unto gentlemen, which, with grazing, frequenting of markets, and keeping servants not idle as the gentleman doth, but such as get both their own living and part of their masters; by these means do come to such wealth that they are able and daily do buy the lands of unthrifty gentlemen, and after setting their sons to the school at the universities, to the law of the realm, or otherwise leaving them sufficient lands whereon they may live without labour, do make their said sons by those means gentlemen. . . .

> Thomas Smith, *De Republica Anglorum*, ed.
> L. Alston (Cambridge, 1906), pp. 41–3

15 The high rewards of trade

It is well known that mercantile fortunes increased dramatically during the Elizabethan period, and Thomas Wilson's estimates of the wealth of some of the leading citizens of Norwich and London are indications of contemporary ideas about the extent of their riches. We now know that Wilson almost certainly exaggerated—London merchants who were worth a good deal less than £50,000 would certainly have been accounted rich men at the time, and very few indeed were worth as much as £100,000—but, though we should moderate his figures, there is no doubt about the reality of the fortunes of the leading townsmen. Their wealth was much more liquid than that of the nobility and gentry, which was tied up in land, and it was this fact which both encouraged and enabled the merchant classes to take the leading role in Elizabethan charitable benefactions. (It is of interest that some of the prosperity of Norwich was based on child labour.)

[People] are not suffered to be idle in their cities as they be in any other parts of Christendom, but every child of 6 or 7 years old is forced to some art whereby he gaineth his own living and something besides to help to enrich his parents or master. I have known in one city viz. Norwich where the accounts having been made yearly what children from 6 to 10 years have earned towards their keeping in a year, and it hath been accounted that it hath risen to 12,000 pounds sterling which they have gained, besides other keeping, and that chiefly by knitting of fine jersey stockings, every child being able at or soon after 7 years to earn 4 shillings a week at that trade, which the merchants uttered at London, and some trading therewith with France and other parts. And in that city I have known in my time 24 aldermen which were esteemed to be worth £20,000 a piece, some much more, and the better sort of citizens the half. But if we should speak of London and some other maritime places we should find it much exceeding this rate. It is well known that at this time there are in London some merchants worth £100,000, and he is not accounted rich that cannot reach to £50,000 or near it. . . .

> T. Wilson, 'The State of England, *anno. dom.* 1600', ed. F. J. Fisher, *Camden Misc.*, xvi (1936), pp. 20–21

16   The yeomen of England

Wilson's figure for the total number of yeomen, 90,000, is probably an underestimate, as his source was the 'sheriffs' books' which were drawn up to provide a list of those eligible for jury service and only contained the names of freeholders. As we have seen, however, not all yeomen were freeholders, and this applied as much to the richer as to the less wealthy members of that class.

Of these yeomen of the richest sort which are able to lend the Queen money (as they do ordinarily upon her letters called privy seals whensoever she hath any wars defensive or offensive or any other enterprise) there are accounted to be about 10,000 in country villages besides citizens.

There are, moreover, of yeomen of meaner ability, which are called freeholders for that they are owners of lands which hold by no base service of any lord or superior, such as are able to keep 10 or 11 or 8 or 6 milk cows, 5 or 6 horses to till their ground, besides young beasts and sheep, and are accounted to be worth each of them in all their substance and stock betwixt 3 and 5 hundred pounds sterling more or less; of these, I say, there are reckoned to be in England and Wales about the number of 80,000, as I have seen in sheriffs' books.

> T. Wilson, 'The State of England, *anno. dom.* 1600', ed. F. J. Fisher, *Camden Misc.*, xvi (1936), p. 19

17 The fourth sort which do not rule

The 'lower orders' in Elizabethan England, those who existed 'only to be ruled', made up the overwhelming majority of the population. They lived just above, or in some cases well below, adequate subsistence levels and the attitude of members of the governing class (like Smith) to such 'low and base persons' was to assume that they knew their place in society.

The fourth sort or class amongst us is of those which the old Romans called *capite*, *censii*, *proletarii*, or *operae*, day labourers, poor husbandmen, yea merchants or retailers which have no free land, copyholders and all artificers, as tailors, shoemakers, carpenters, brickmakers, bricklayers, masons, etc. These have no voice nor authority in our commonwealth, and no account is made of them but only to be ruled, not to rule other; and yet they be not altogether neglected. For in cities and corporate towns for default of yeomen, inquests and juries are impanelled of such manner of people. And in villages they be commonly made churchwardens, alecunners, and many times constables, which office toucheth more the commonwealth, and at first was not employed upon such low and base persons.

Thomas Smith, *De Republica Anglorum*, ed.
L. Alston (Cambridge, 1906), p. 46

18 Life of the lower orders

This excerpt from Harrison makes it plain that, although in prosperous times husbandmen and artificers might enjoy a very adequate and varied diet, such relative good living could never be taken for granted. In times of scarcity they had to make do with 'horsecorn' bread, and, indeed, in very severe conditions the poorest might even starve to death, as certainly happened in the midlands during the famine years of the mid 1590s.

The artificer and husbandman make greatest account of such meat as they may soonest come by, and have it quickliest ready.... Their food also consisteth principally in beef, and such meat as the butcher selleth, that is to say, mutton, veal, lamb, pork, etc., whereof he [i.e. the artificer] findeth great store in the markets adjoining, beside souse, brawn, bacon, fruit, pies of fruit, fowls of sundry sorts, cheese, butter, eggs, etc.... In feasting also, this latter sort, I mean the husbandmen, do exceed after their manner, especially at bridals, purifications of women and such odd meetings where it is incredible to tell what meat is consumed and spent, each one bringing such a dish or so many with him as his wife and he do consult upon. . . . To conclude, both the artificer and the husbandman are sufficiently liberal and very friendly at their tables; and when they meet they are so merry without malice, and plain without inward Italian or French craft and subtlety, that it would do a man good to be in company among them. Herein only are the inferior sort somewhat to be blamed, that being thus assembled, their talk is now and then such as savoureth of scurrility and ribaldry, a thing naturally incident to carters and clowns, who think themselves not to be merry and welcome, if their foolish veins in this behalf be never so little restrained. . . .

The bread throughout the land is made of such grain as the soil yieldeth, nevertheless the gentility commonly provide themselves sufficiently of wheat for their own tables, whilst their household and poor neighbours in some shires are enforced to content themselves with rye, or barley, yea, and in time of dearth many with bread made either of beans, peas, or oats, or of all together and some acorns among, of which scourge the poorest do soonest taste, since they are least able to provide themselves of better. I will not say that this extremity is oft so well to be seen in time of plenty as of dearth, but if I should, I could easily bring my trial. For albeit that there be much more ground eared now almost in every place than hath been of late years, yet such a price of corn continueth in each town and market . . . that the artificer and poor labouring man is not able to reach unto it, but is driven to content himself with horsecorn, I mean beans, peas, oats, tares and lintels: and therefore it is a true proverb and never so well verified as now, that 'hunger setteth his first foot into the horse manger.' If the world last a while after this rate, wheat and rye will be no grain for poor men to feed on. . . .

W. Harrison, *Description of England*, ed.
F. J. Furnivall (1877), i, 150–51, 153

19 The poor

Throughout the Tudor period there were numerous complaints about the great and growing numbers of the poor. Some of these accounts are doubtless exaggerated, but it seems clear that the numbers of vagabonds and of the poor did increase in the sixteenth century. There were many reasons for this. Lambarde, a notable scholar who wrote *Eirenarcha*, the classic Elizabethan book on the justices of the peace, described some which seemed important to him in this speech, made in 1594. He drew particular attention to the effects of the war in the later years of Elizabeth's reign, but made no reference to what historians would now agree was the main cause: the pressure of a growing population—it increased from about 2½ to perhaps 4 millions in the sixteenth century—upon limited resources. This produced unemployment as well as a situation in which prices rose more rapidly than wages, with disastrous consequences for the poorer sections of the population. (In the sixteenth century dearth retained its original meaning of dearness, but it was, of course, a reflection of scarcity in its modern sense.)

The dearth of all things maketh likewise many poor, and that cometh either by the excessive enhancement of the rents of land, which hath now invaded the lands both of the church and Crown itself, or by that foul and cancerous sore of daily usury, which is already run and spread over all the body of the commonwealth, or by our immoderate use, or rather abuse, of foreign commodities, the which we (breaking all symmetry and good proportion) do make as vile and common unto us as our own domestical. But whether these only, or chiefly, or they with some other be the true causes of dearth, that is a disputation for another time, place, and assembly. These I note that every man may have a conscience in them, lest through his fault dearth grow and consequently the number of the poor be increased by it.

Lastly, the poor are exceedingly much multiplied because for the most part all the whole children and brood of the poor be poor also, seeing that they are not taken from their wandering parents and brought up to honest labour for their living but, following their idle steps . . . , as they be born and brought up, so do they live and die, most shameless and shameful rogues and beggars.

And to the increase of these evils we have, as I said, a sort of poor lately crept in amongst us and not before known to our elders: I mean poor soldiers, of whom this commission specially speaketh. There were always poor leprous, poor lazarous, aged poor, sick poor, poor widows, poor orphans, and suchlike, but poor soldiers were either rarely or never heard of till now of late. And this is the reason: not only in old time but also within the reach of our own memories . . . the nobility, knighthood, and gentry of the realm carried to the wars with them their freehold or copyhold tenants, their able and wealthy neighbours, and their own menial and household servants, of which three sorts two were able at their return to live of their own and the third was never forsaken of their lords and masters under whom they had adventured. But now, when not only our gaols are scoured and our highways swept but also the cannels [i.e. channels] of our streets be raked for soldiers, what marvel is it if after their return from the wars they do either lead their lives in begging or end them by hanging. Nevertheless we are by many duties most bounden to help and relieve them, considering that they fight for the truth of God and defense of their country; yea, they fight our own war and do serve in our places, enduring cold and hunger when we live at ease and fare well, lying in the open field when we are lodged in our beds of down, and meeting with broken heads and limbs when we find it good and safe sleeping in a whole skin.

William Lambarde and Local Government, ed. C. Read, Folger Shakespeare Library (Ithaca, 1962), pp. 182–4

20   Regulations about dress

In previous excerpts we have examined the Elizabethan social classes from the nobility at one end of the scale to the poor at the other. Contemporaries believed that there was an appropriate dress suitable for each of these different orders of society. In the Middle Ages and during the early Tudor period monarchs had sought to regulate dress by statutes and proclamations, prohibiting their subjects from wearing specified clothes unless they were of a certain rank. During Elizabeth's reign there was no new legislation on the subject, but the Queen did her best to enforce existing statutes by a series of proclamations, issued at intervals throughout her reign. The one below includes a schedule which sets out the provisions of the two most important early Tudor enactments on the subject, the statutes of 1533 and 1554. Like all the later proclamations of the reign on this subject this seems to have been honoured as much in the breach as in the observance, and foreign and native commentators alike are unanimous in their accounts of the extravagant attire of both men and women of all but the poorest classes. In such a situation, where the growing wealth of the country enabled large numbers to dress above their station, the persistent attempts of the rigorously conservative Elizabeth to enforce the statutes of apparel were foredoomed to failure.

First her majesty's said Council, by her commandment, shall and will presently take order that the statute made in the first and second years of King Philip and Queen Mary, and certain other branches of another statute made the 24th year of King Henry VIII, against excessive apparel, shall be put in execution, both within her majesty's court and in their own houses, with a certain favorable proceeding touching such as can not presently, without their overgreat loss, change their unlawful apparel which they presently have. Wherein because her majesty trusteth that the example shall induce the rest of her subjects to reform their disorders: her majesty hath willed her said Privy Council to publish by her authority their decree and order in this behalf.

And for like toleration toward such as live in the country out of her court, her majesty chargeth forthwith all mayors and governors of cities and towns corporate, all sheriffs and justices of peace in shires, all noblemen of the estate of barons and above, all governors and heads of any societies and companies, either ecclesiastical or temporal, forthwith, or at the furthest within the space of 12 days after the publication hereof, to devise, accord, and take order, either according to the example of her majesty's council, or else after some other better manner, as the place shall require, for the execution of the foresaid statute and branches, specified hereafter in a brief abstract and draft annexed to this proclamation, within the limit of their charge; so as her majesty may take some comfort of her toleration, and the commonwealth some relief of the great damage hereby sustained. Wherein if her majesty shall see her expectation deceived, she shall thereby have just occasion to proceed with execution of her laws, both to the benefit of her commonweal and to the chastisement of such disordered subjects as, being favourably warned, will not amend. Which thing her majesty purposeth certainly to do in more effectual sort than heretofore hath been.

And because the toleration of these abuses shall not be drawn to any sinister occasion of continuance of this abuse, her majesty chargeth and commandeth that there be no toleration had, nor excuse allowed, after the 20th day of December next as touching all the contents of the said statute in the 1st and 2nd years of King Philip and Queen Mary, neither after the last of January next as touching the branches of the other statute of the 24th year of King Henry VIII, noted hereafter in the end of this proclamation, other than is contained in the same statutes and branches; except it be for certain costly furs and rich embroideries bought and made by sundry gentlemen before this proclamation, to their great costs, with which her highness is pleased to dispense.

THE BRIEF CONTENT OF CERTAIN ACTS OF PARLIAMENT AGAINST THE INORDINATE USE OF APPAREL
24 HENRY VIII

None shall wear in his apparel any:

cloth of gold, silver, or tinsel; satin, silk, or cloth mixed with gold or silver, nor any sables; except earls and all of superior degrees, and viscounts and barons in their doublets and sleeveless coats;

woollen cloth made out of the realm; velvet, crimson, scarlet, or blue;

furs, black genets, lucerns; except dukes, marquises, earls or their children, barons, and knights of the order [of the garter];

velvet in gowns, coats, or outermost garments, furs of leopards; embroidery; pricking or printing with gold, silver, or silk; except barons' sons, knights, or men that may dispend £200 by year; taffeta, satin, damask, or silk camlet in his outermost garments; velvet, otherwise than in jackets, doublets, etc.; fur whereof the kind groweth not within the Queen's dominions, except gray genets, bodge; except a man that may dispend £100 by year.

1 & 2 PHILIP AND MARY

None shall wear any silk in ·

hat, bonnet, nightcap, girdle, scabbard, hose, shoes, spur leathers; except the son and heir or daughter of a knight, or the wife of the said son, a man that may dispend £20 by year, or is worth £200 in goods.

> Proclamation enforcing statutes of apparel, 21 October 1559, *Tudor Royal Proclamations*, ed. P. L. Hughes and J. F. Larkin (New Haven, 1969), ii, 136–8

21 Violent change among the English

This hostile 'character study' of the English people, written by a Venetian diplomat at the beginning of Elizabeth's reign, stresses two features of contemporary life which impressed many observers: rapid change and violence. It should be borne in mind that this passage was written at the time of greatest change when, within thirty years England had altered the established faith four times.

The English are universally partial to novelty, hostile to foreigners, and not very friendly amongst themselves; they attempt to do everything that comes into their heads, just as if all that the imagination suggests could be easily executed; hence a greater number of insurrections have broken out in this country than in all the rest of the world, the most recent of these being that raised by Thomas Stafford, nephew of the Cardinal [Pole], who endeavoured to obtain the kingdom with only sixty men brought by him from France, and he paid the penalty of his temerity.

From the same cause has arisen the change of faith, which is the greatest alteration that could possibly arise in a nation, because besides the offence which is thus committed against our Lord God, a revolution in customs, laws, obedience, and, lastly, in the very state itself necessarily follows, as has happened in . . . a great part of Europe.

Hence also have resulted many depositions of great men and promotions of the unworthy, many imprisonments, exiles, and deaths. It is also a fact, incredible though true, namely, that during the last twenty years three Princes of the blood, four Dukes, forty earls, and more than three thousand other persons have died by violent death. It may therefore be easily imagined that no foreigner could rule this kind of people, when even their own countrymen are not safe.

> Report by Michiel Soriano to the Signory, probably written in 1559, *Cal. S.P. Venetian 1558–80*, p. 328

22   The English character

The following account, written by a merchant from Antwerp who lived in London during Elizabeth's reign, stresses, in common with the previous excerpt, the violence and xenophobia of the English. It also describes their immense capacity for eating: sixteenth-century Englishmen seem to have acquired something of a reputation for gluttony among foreigners.

The people are bold, courageous, ardent, and cruel in war, fiery in attack, and having little fear of death. They are not vindictive, but very inconstant, rash, vainglorious, light and deceiving, and very suspicious, especially of foreigners, whom they despise. They are full of courtly and affected manners and words, which they take for gentility, civility, and wisdom. They are eloquent and very hospitable; they feed well and delicately, and eat a great deal of meat; and as the Germans pass the bounds of sobriety in drinking, these do the same in eating, for which the fertility of the country affords them sufficient means, although in general the fruits have not such strength and virtue as in France or the Netherlands for the want of hot sun. Even the grass, as the herbalists say, is not so nourishing, whereby the meat is in consequence softer and not so firm, although they have a great abundance of it; but it is well-tasted enough.

> Account of the English by Emanuel van Meteren, in W. B. Rye, *England as seen by foreigners in the days of Elizabeth and James I* (1865), p. 70

23 The fair sex

This account of English women, written by a perceptive foreigner in 1575, is particularly interesting because of its favourable tone. Contemporary English commentators, like William Harrison, had some harsh things to say about their fellow countrywomen, particularly about their love for extravagant clothes.

The women are beautiful, fair, well dressed and modest, which is seen there more than elsewhere, as they go about the streets without any covering ... of ... mantle, hood, veil or the like. Married women only wear a hat both in the street and in the house; those unmarried go without a hat, although ladies of distinction have lately learnt to cover their faces with silken masks or vizards, and feathers—for indeed they change very easily and that every year, to the astonishment of many.

> Account of the English by Emanuel van Meteren, in W. B. Rye, *England as seen by foreigners in the days of Elizabeth and James I* (1865), p. 73

24 The people of London

This account of late Elizabethan London by a visiting German prince stresses again some notable features of English life at the time, the chauvinism and violence of the inhabitants in general and the splendid attire of the women. His comments on the populousness of the City are worth noting. London expanded at a tremendous rate during the Elizabethan period, when it certainly more than doubled its population, reaching a figure of well over 200,000 by 1603.

[London] is a very populous city, so that one can scarcely pass along the streets, on account of the throng.

The inhabitants are magnificently apparelled, and are extremely proud and overbearing; and because the greater part, especially the trades people, seldom go into other countries, but always remain in their houses in the city attending to their business, they care little for foreigners, but scoff and laugh at them; and moreover one dare not oppose them, else the streetboys and apprentices collect together in immense crowds and strike to the right and left unmercifully without regard to person; and because they are the strongest, one is obliged to put up with the insult as well as the injury.

The women have much more liberty than perhaps in any other

place. They also know well how to make use of it, for they go dressed out in exceedingly fine clothes, and give all their attention to their ruffs and stuffs, to such a degree indeed, that, as I am informed, many a one does not hesitate to wear velvet in the streets, which is common with them, whilst at home perhaps they have not a piece of dry bread.

> Account of the visit of Frederick, Duke of Württemberg to England in 1592, in W. B. Rye, *England as seen by foreigners in the days of Elizabeth and James 1* (1865), pp. 7–8

25 The trades of London

John Stow, one of the most notable of the distinguished antiquaries of the Elizabethan period, wrote an exhaustive and invaluable *Survey of London*, first published in 1598. This excerpt gives some idea of the great variety of trades which flourished in the City in Elizabeth's reign.

Men of trades and sellers of wares in this city have oftentimes changed their places, as they have found their best advantage. For whereas Mercers and Haberdashers used to keep their shops in West Cheap, of later time they held them on London Bridge, where partly they yet remain. The Goldsmiths of Gutherons-lane and Old Exchange are now for the most part removed into the south side of West Cheap; the Pepperers and Grocers of Sopers-lane are now in Bucklersbury and other places dispersed. The Drapers of Lombard-street and of Cornhill are seated in Candlewick-street and Watling-street; the Skinners from St. Mary Pellipers or at the Axe into Budge-row and Walbrook; the Stockfishmongers in Thames-street, Wet-fishmongers in Knightriders-street and Bridge-street; the Ironmongers of Ironmongers-lane and Old Jewry into Thames-street; the Vintners from the Vinetree into divers places. But the Brewers for the most part remain near to the friendly water of Thames; the Butchers in Eastcheap, St. Nicholas Shambles and the Stocks Market. The Hosiers of old time in Hosier-lane, near unto Smithfield, are since removed into Cordwainer-street, the upper part thereof by Bow Church, and last of all into Birchovers-lane by Corn-hill. The Shoemakers and Curriers of Cordwainer-street removed the one to St. Martins-le-Grand, the other to London Wall near unto Moorgate. . . . Cooks or Pastelars for the more part in Thames-street, the other dispersed into divers parts. Poulters of late removed out of the Pountry betwixt the Stocks and the Great Conduit in Cheap into Grass-street and St. Nicholas Shambles; Bowyers from Bowyers-row

by Ludgate into divers places, and almost worn out with the Fletchers.
. . . Patten-makers of St. Margaret, Pattens-lane, clean worn out.

> J. Stow, *A Survey of London*, ed. C. L. Kings-
> ford (Oxford, 1908), i, 81

26   A sixteenth-century traffic problem

In this passage, Stow makes it plain that Elizabethan London had an acute
traffic problem. This was caused partly by the great increase in the population
of the City, but also by the general rise in living standards among sections of
the upper classes, which was such a feature of the Elizabethan period. Many
more people than before could afford coaches and those who could bought
them as status symbols as much as for personal convenience.

The number of cars, drays, carts and coaches more than hath been
accustomed, the streets and lanes being straitened, must needs be
dangerous, as daily experience proveth. The coachman rides behind the
horse tails, lasheth them and looketh not behind him; the drayman
sitteth and sleepeth on his dray and letteth his horse lead him home. I
know that by the good laws and customs of this city shod carts are
forbidden to enter the same, except upon reasonable causes, as service
of the prince or suchlike, they be tolerated; also that the fore-horse of
every carriage should be led by hand—but these good orders are not
observed. . . . Now of late years the use of coaches brought out of
Germany is taken up and made so common as there is neither distinction of time nor difference of persons observed; for the world runs on
wheels with many whose parents were glad to go on foot.

> J. Stow, *A Survey of London*, ed. C. L. Kings-
> ford (Oxford, 1908), i, 83–4

27   Rough stuff and the aftermath

This passage from a letter written by Recorder Fleetwood to Lord Burghley
during the summer of 1584 shows how quickly tempers could get out of hand
in Elizabethan London. It is clear that the incident began as a minor quarrel, but
it soon escalated into a full scale riot, with a crowd of 300 attacking Lyon's inn,
one of the lesser institutions for legal studies attached to the more important
Inner Temple. This is a good illustration of why both central and local government were so preoccupied with disturbances of any kind. They could easily
get out of hand when there was no professional police force or standing army to
deal with violent trouble.

Upon the same Wednesday at night two companions, one being a tailor and the other a clerk of the common pleas . . . , and both very lewd fellows, fell out about an harlot, and the tailor raised the prentices and other light persons and, thinking that the clerk was run into Lyon's Inn, came to the house with three hundred at the least, brake down the windows of the house, and struck at the gentlemen, during which broil one Randolds a baker's son came into Fleet street and there made solemn proclamation for 'clubs'. The street rose and took and brought him unto me and the next day we indicted him also for his misdemeanour with many other more.

Upon Wednesday, Thursday, Friday and Saturday we did nothing else but sit in commission and examine these misdemeanours. . . .

> Recorder Fleetwood to Lord Burghley, 18 June 1584, in J. Dover Wilson, *Life in Shakespeare's England* (Pelican ed., 1944), p. 102

28 Alms for the poor

This contemporary account of the poor prisoners of Newgate brings out the harsh fate of the poor inside prison, at a time when rich prisoners were often allowed to live in considerable style, having good food brought in to them and many of their personal possessions around them.

In London, and other such places, it would move a stony heart to hear one crying up and down the streets, 'Bread and meat for the poor prisoners of Newgate, for Christ Jesus' sake!', and the prisoners crying out of their grates and holes, 'One penny or half-penny, for Christ his sake, to buy some bread, to buy some bread!'

> W. Burton, 'The rowsing of the sluggard' (1595), in A. Nicoll, *The Elizabethans* (Cambridge, 1957), p. 49

29 The curse of war

This passage comes from a speech made by Lambarde in 1586 at Kent Quarter Sessions. The war which he refers to is, of course, the war with Spain which began in 1585, when the Queen despatched an English force to the Netherlands to help the Dutch in their struggle against Spain. She was also for the rest of her reign embroiled in Ireland. Lambarde's fears about the effects of these military operations were amply confirmed in the 1590s when, during a period of acute social distress caused partly by bad harvests, large numbers of discharged

soldiers and mariners, or rogues pretending to be soldiers and mariners, terror-
ised whole areas of the countryside.

. . . it must be confessed that this, as all other wars, will bring the
wonted evils and companions of war and hostility with it. For now
such men as have more valour in their bodies than virtue in their minds
will think that all the labour lieth on their hands and will therefore
grow insolent and boldly adventure upon the breach of laws in hope
that (for the necessity that we have of their service) they may not only
escape punishment but pass without controlment for it. Now will your
sons and servants strive to draw their necks out of the yoke of due
obedience. Now will loiterers and idle persons think themselves
warranted to walk at their wills. Now will beastly drunkards and
blasphemers vaunt that they be valiant and serviceable men. Yea, now
will thieves and robbers take upon them as if they were the only
soldiers of the world.

> *William Lambarde and Local Government*, ed.
> C. Read, Folger Shakespeare Library (Ithaca,
> 1962), pp. 83–4

30 The threat of the plague, 1593

Epidemics of plague were common in Elizabethan England and were often at
their most severe in London. This was true of the plague of 1563, the first
serious outbreak of Elizabeth's reign, and also of that of 1592–3, when many
thousands died in the capital alone. This proclamation shows the concern of the
Queen and her advisers that every possible measure should be taken to prevent
the disease from spreading to the royal household.

The Queen's Majesty, being duly informed how greatly and in many
places the infection of the sickness is at this time dispersed, by reason
whereof her highness in her princely care and wisdom weighing the
danger thereof, and how necessary it is to have restraint made of haunt
and repair to her majesty's court, doth upon this good consideration,
and that her court may (with God's favor) be the better preserved from
infection, charge and command that no manner persons but such as
have cause to remain or come to her court for their ordinary attendance
upon her majesty's person, or to do service in her court, shall make their
repair to her court or within two miles of the same; upon pain to be
committed to prison for their contempt.

> *Tudor Royal Proclamations*, ed. P. L. Hughes
> and J. F. Larkin (New Haven, 1969), iii,
> 121

31   Famine

Shakespeare's *Midsummer Night's Dream* was composed in the mid 1590s and this excerpt from a speech by Titania is usually taken to refer to the harvest crisis of these years, which was the most important element in creating the disastrous situation of the period, which included a severe threat to general law and order and to social stability.

> The ox hath therefore stretch'd his yoke in vain,
> The ploughman lost his sweat, and the green corn
> Hath rotted ere his youth attain'd a beard;
> The fold stands empty in the drowned field,
> And crows are fatted with the murrion flock;
> The nine men's morris is fill'd up with mud,
> And the quaint mazes in the wanton green,
> For lack of tread, are undistinguishable.
> The human mortals want their winter here;
> No night is now with hymn or carol blest;
> Therefore the moon, the governess of floods,
> Pale in her anger, washes all the air,
> That rheumatic diseases do abound.
> And through this distemperature we see
> The seasons alter: hoary-headed frosts
> Fall in the fresh lap of the crimson rose . . .
> . . . The spring, the summer,
> The childing autumn, angry winter, change
> Their wonted liveries; and the mazed world,
> By their increase, now knows not which is which.

> W. Shakespeare, *A Midsummer Night's Dream*, II. S i, 93–108, 111–14

32   Colonial plans

Some leading Elizabethans, troubled though they were by war, plague and famine, aimed at gaining a hold on the New World by establishing English colonies on the other side of the Atlantic. Richard Hakluyt was one of the greatest Elizabethan colonial propagandists and these notes show the practical sense with which he approached the problems of permanent settlement abroad. Although none of the sixteenth-century plantations took root, the Elizabethans' colonial visions began to be realised with the establishment of Virginia in James I's reign.

That the first seat be chosen on the seaside so as (if it may be) you may have your own navy within bay, river or lake, within your seat safe from the enemy. And so as the enemy shall be forced to lie in open road abroad without, to be dispersed with all winds and tempests that shall arise. Thus seated you shall be least subject to annoy of the enemy, so may you by your navy within, pass out to all parts of the world, and so may the ships of England have access to you to supply all wants, so may your commodities be carried away also. This seat is to be chosen in temperate climate, in sweet air, where you may possess always sweet water, wood, sea-coals, or turf, with fish, flesh, grain, fruits, herbs and roots, or so many of those, as may suffice very necessity for the life of such as shall plant there. And for the possessing of mines of gold, of silver, copper, quicksilver, or of any such precious thing, the wants of divers of those needful things may be supplied from some other place by sea, etcetera.

Stone to make lime of.
Slate stone to tile withal or such clay as makes tile,
Stone to wall withal if brick may not be made,
Timber for building easily to be conveyed to the place,
Reed to cover houses or such like, if tile or slate be not.

are to be looked for as things without which no city may be made nor people in civil sort be kept together.

The people there to plant and to continue are either to live without traffic, or by traffic and by trade of merchandise. If they shall live without sea traffic, at the first they become naked by want of linen and woollen, and very miserable by infinite wants that will otherwise ensue, and so will they be forced of themselves to depart, or else easily they will be consumed by the Spaniards, by the French or by the natural inhabitants of the country, and so the enterprise becomes reproachful to our nation, and a let to many other good purposes that may be taken in hand.

And by trade of merchandise they can not live, except the sea or the land there may yield commodity for commodity. And therefore you ought to have most special regard of that point, and so to plant, that the natural commodities of the place and seat may draw to you access of navigation for the same, or that by your own navigation you may carry the same out, and fetch home the supply of the wants of the seat.

Richard Hakluyt's notes on Colonisation, in
*The Voyages and Colonial Enterprises of Sir
Humphrey Gilbert*, ed. D. B. Quinn (Hakluyt
Soc., 2nd ser., lxxxiii, 1938), pp. 151–2

33 Red Indians and how to tame them

The Elizabethans' colonial voyages brought them into contact with a people at a very different level of civilisation from their own—the 'Indians' of the New World, as is illustrated by the account written in 1588 by Thomas Hariot, the eminent mathematician, astronomer and explorer.

They are a people clothed with loose mantles made of deer skins, and aprons of the same round about their middles; all else naked. . . . [They have] no edge tools or weapons of iron or steel to offend us withall, neither know they how to make any: those weapons that they have, are only bows made of witch-hazel, and arrows of reeds, flat edged truncheons also of wood about a yard long, neither have they any thing to defend themselves but targets made of barks, and some armours made of sticks wickered together with thread.

Their towns are but small, and near the sea coast but few, some containing but 10 or 12 houses, some 20, the greatest that we have seen have been but of 30 houses: if they be walled it is only done with barks of trees made fast to stakes, or else with poles only fixed upright and close one by another. . . .

. . . Their manner of wars amongst themselves is either by sudden surprising one another most commonly about the dawning of the day, or moonlight, or else by ambushes, or some subtle devices. Set battles are very rare, except it fall out where there are many trees, where either part may have some hope of defence, after the delivery of every arrow, in leaping behind some or other.

If there fall out any wars between us and them, what their fight is likely to be, we having advantages against them so many manner of ways, as by our discipline, our strange weapons and devices else, especially by ordnance great and small, it may be easily imagined; by the experience we have had in some places, the turning up of their heels against us in running away was their best defence. In respect of us they are a people poor, and for want of skill and judgement in the knowledge and use of our things, do esteem our trifles before things of greater value: notwithstanding, in their proper manner, considering the want of such means as we have, they seem very ingenious; for although they have no such tools, nor any such crafts, sciences and arts as we, yet in those things they do, they show excellency of wit. And by how much they upon due consideration shall find our manner of knowledges and crafts to exceed theirs in perfection, and speed for doing or execution, by so much the more is it probable that they should desire our friendship and love, and have the greater respect for pleasing and obeying us. Whereby may be hoped, if means of good government be used, that they may in short time be brought to civility, and the embracing of true religion.

Some religion they have already, which although it be far from the truth, yet being as it is, there is hope it may be the easier and sooner reformed.

> Thomas Hariot, 'A Brief and True Report', *The Roanoke Voyages*, *1584–90*, ed. D. B. Quinn (Hakluyt Soc., 2nd ser., civ, 1955), i, 368–72

34   *Vive le sport!*

Lord Herbert of Cherbury (1583–1648) wrote a notable autobiography which was first published in the eighteenth century. The most distinctive characteristics of the book as a whole are its fascinating details, not always accurate, and the immense vanity of the author. Herbert represents himself as gay, handsome and brave, an idol of the ladies who was equally acclaimed and respected by men. In this passage he does, however, give a fairly accurate account of the kind of sports which were widespread among the gentry.

That dancing may be learnt first, as that which doth fashion the body gives one a good presence in and address to all companies, since it disposeth the limbs to a kind of *souplesse* (as the Frenchmen call it) and agility, insomuch as they seem to have the use of their legs, arms and bodies, more than any others, who, standing stiff and stark in their postures, seem as if they were taken in their joints, or had not the perfect use of their members. . . .

. . . The next exercise a young man should learn (but not before he is eleven or twelve years of age) is fencing; for the attaining of which the Frenchman's rule is excellent, *bon pied bon oeil*, by which to teach men how far they may stretch out their feet when they would make a thrust against their enemy, lest either should overstride themselves, or, not striding far enough, fail to bring the point of their weapon home. The second part of his direction adviseth the scholar to keep a fixed eye upon the point of his enemy's sword, to the intent he may both put by or ward the blows and thrusts made against him, and together direct the point of his sword upon some part of his enemy that lieth naked and open to him.

... I spent much time also in learning to ride the great horse, that creature being made above all others for the service of man, as giving his rider all the advantages of which he is capable, while sometimes he gives him strength, sometimes agility or motion for the overcoming of his enemy, insomuch, that a good rider on a good horse, is as much above himself and others, as his world can make him. ...

... It will be fit for a gentleman also to learn to swim, unless he be given to cramps and convulsions; howbeit, I must confess, in my own particular, that I cannot swim; for, as I was once in danger of drowning, by learning to swim, my mother, upon her blessing, charged me never to learn swimming, telling me further, that she had heard of more drowned than saved by it; which reason, though it did not prevail with me, yet her commandment did. It will be good also for a gentleman to learn to leap, wrestle, and vault on horseback; they being all of them qualities of great use. I do much approve likewise of shooting in the long-bow, as being both an healthful exercise and useful for the wars, notwithstanding all that our firemen speak against it; for, bring an hundred archers against so many musqueteers, I say if the archer comes within his distance, he will not only make two shoots, but two hits for one.

The exercises I do not approve of are riding of running horses, there being much cheating in that kind; neither do I see why a brave man should delight in a creature whose chief use is to help him to run away. I do not much like of hunting horses, that exercise taking up more time than can be spared from a man studious to get knowledge; it is enough, therefore, to know the sport, if there be any in it, without making it an ordinary practice; and, indeed, of the two, hawking is the better, because less time is spent in it. And upon these terms also I can allow a little bowling; so that the company be choice and good.

The exercises I wholly condemn, are dicing and carding, especially if you play for any great sum of money, or spend any time in them; or use to come to meetings in dicing-houses where cheaters meet and cozen young gentlemen of all their money.

The Autobiography of Edward, Lord Herbert of Cherbury, ed. S. L. Lee (1886), pp. 70–79

35 The language

The Elizabethan period was one of the great eras in the development of the English language, a fact which Harrison proclaimed very clearly in this passage. He was right to draw attention to the importance of contemporary

English writers in the process—though the greatest of all, William Shakespeare, had not produced his plays when Harrison wrote—but was wrong in condemning the importation of foreign words, which, in fact, did much to enrich Elizabethan English. It is worth remembering too that local variations of speech were much more pronounced then than they are now. For example, it might have been difficult for a man from a different part of the country to understand Sir Walter Raleigh, who spoke 'broad Devonshire' all his life. Note too, that in Wales, then as now, the Welsh language spoken in the north was considered superior to that of the south.

. . . our said tongue was brought to an excellent pass, notwithstanding that it never came unto the type of perfection until the time of Queen Elizabeth, wherein John Jewel, Bishop of Sarum, John Foxe, and sundry learned and excellent writers have fully accomplished the ornature of the same, to their great praise and immortal commendation, although not a few other do greatly seek to stain the same by fond affectation of foreign and strange words, presuming that to be the best English which is most corrupted with external [foreign] terms of eloquence and found of many syllables.

But as this excellency of the English tongue is found in one, and the south, part of this island, so in Wales the greatest number (as I said) retain still their own ancient language, that of the north part of the said country being less corrupted than the other, and therefore reputed for the better in their own estimation and judgment.

W. Harrison, *Description of England*, ed.
F. J. Furnivall (1877), i, xxx

II

THE ECONOMY

1 Troubled and dangerous times

This brief note by a government official, written early in the reign, reveals something of the grim situation confronting the Queen. However, though he writes alarmingly of military weakness, high prices and extravagant living, he makes no mention of the weakness of the enemy. For example, the French king's power was, in part, illusory: he was at the end of a long exhausting struggle with Spain, and his grasp on Scotland was very insecure. He was soon to be driven from Scotland, but Calais was lost to England for ever.

The queen poor, the realm exhausted, the nobility poor and decayed. Want of good captains and soldiers. The people out of order. Justice not executed. All things dear. Excess in meat, drink and apparel. Divisions among ourselves. Wars with France and Scotland. The French king bestriding the realm, having one foot in Calais and the other in Scotland. Steadfast enmity but no steadfast friendship abroad.

ARMIGAIL WAAD, CLERK OF THE COUNCIL.
Cited in C. Read, *Mr. Secretary Cecil and Queen Elizabeth* (1955), p. 124

2 Inflation

Since the great debasement of the coinage by Henry VIII in 1544, the whole currency situation had become increasingly confused, its worst period being under Edward VI. Various attempts to restore the purity had failed, through the greed, inexperience and inefficiency of some of the ministers involved. The major attempt, inaugurated by this proclamation of September 1560, proved a more skilful operation, with careful timing and firm dates as to when the base currency would cease to be legal tender. Much of the success was due to the Queen's financial agent, Sir Thomas Gresham—though he subsequently exaggerated his achievement—and to the support of the merchants of London. Nonetheless, the fundamental causes of inflation, deriving from the population crisis, could not be eliminated by this measure.

The Queen's Most Excellent Majesty, amongst other great and weighty consultations had at sundry times with her council and sometimes with other wise and expert men for the reformation of such abuses as be thought hurtful to the commonweal of this her realm, hath found by consent of all sorts of wise men that nothing is so grievous nor likely to disturb and decay the state and good order of this realm as the sufferance of the base moneys (being of divers standards and mixtures) to be so abundantly current within this realm, which have been coined in the same before her majesty's reign and no part since; nor contrariwise any one thing so profitable, or in short time to be so comfortable for all manner of people, as to have in place of the same base and copper moneys fine and good sterling moneys of silver and gold. For her majesty well perceiveth, by the long sufferance of the said base and copper moneys, not only her crown, nobility, and subjects of this her realm to be daily more and more impoverished, the ancient and singular honour and estimation which this realm of England had beyond all other by plenty of moneys of gold and silver, only fine and not base, is hereby decayed and vanished away, but also by reason of these said base moneys great quantity of forged and counterfeits have been and be daily made and brought from beyond the seas, for the which the ancient fine gold and silver and the rich merchandise of this realm is transported and daily carried out of the same to the impoverishing thereof and enriching of others. And finally hereby all manner of prices of things in this realm necessary for sustentation of the people grow daily excessive, to the lamentable and manifest hurt and oppression of the state, specially of pensioners, soldiers, and all hired servants and other mean people that live by any kind of wages and not by rents of lands or trade of merchandise.

> Proclamation devaluing base coins, 27 September 1560, in *Tudor Royal Proclamations*, ed. P. L. Hughes and J. F. Larkin (1969), ii, 150–51

3 'The overgrown number of us'

William Lambarde, historian of Kent, antiquarian, parliamentarian, justice of the peace, here sets out his explanation for the increase of population. Demographers are still uncertain about the degree of increase or its causes. If the full explanation is ever known it is likely to be more complex than Lambarde's. The irony of this passage is that, in the years immediately following, there were in succession three severe famines (cf. no. 12) and the reign ended in a time of plague.

That the number of our people is multiplied, it is both demonstrable to the eye and evident in reason, considering on the one side that nowadays not only young folks of all sorts but churchmen also of each degree do marry and multiply at liberty, which was not wont to be, and on the other side that we have not, God be thanked, been touched with any extreme mortality, either by sword or sickness, that might abate the overgrown number of us. And if all, then each sort, and in them the poorer sort also, must needs be augmented.

> Lambarde's charge at the commission for almshouses, etc., at Maidstone, 17 January 1594, *William Lambarde and Local Government*, ed. C. Read, p. 182

4 The virtues of the plough

A good example, from a preamble to a late Elizabethan Act, of the official conception of the role of agriculture in the economy: to maintain and increase the population; to keep people employed rather than corrupted by idleness; to preserve social stability by a wide dispersion of the national wealth; and to preserve the independence of England by enabling it to live on its own resources.

Whereas the strength and flourishing estate of this kingdom hath been always and is greatly upheld and advanced by the maintenance of the plough and tillage, being the occasion of the increase and multiplying of people both for service in the wars and in times of peace, being also a principal mean that people are set on work, and thereby withdrawn from idleness, drunkenness, unlawful games and all other lewd practices and conditions of life; and whereas by the same means of tillage and husbandry the greater part of the subjects are preserved from extreme poverty in a competent estate of maintenance and means to live, and the wealth of the realm is kept dispersed and distributed in many hands, where it is more ready to answer all necessary charges for the service of the realm; and whereas also the said husbandry and tillage is a cause that the realm doth more stand upon itself, without depending upon foreign countries either for bringing in of corn in time of scarcity, or for vent and utterance of our own commodities being in over-great abundance; . . .

> 39 Eliz. c. 2 (1598), *Statutes of the Realm*, iv, 893

5 The claims of husbandry

This clause from the Statute of Artificers, 1563, a measure which has been much debated among historians as to its authors and purposes, indicates those industries which are regarded as of national importance and which therefore exempt a man from being required to work in agriculture. These include fishing and shipping, food distribution for London, mining and metallurgy and apprenticeship in cities and towns (but not in the new centres of industry springing up in various places). Exemption is also granted on the basis of class: gentlemen and owners of lands and goods of certain values are specifically excluded. So, too, are university students. All the rest are liable to be bound for a year's service in agriculture. (For a further extract from the statute see II. 13 below.)

. . . Every person between the age of twelve years and the age of three score years, not being lawfully retained, nor apprentice with any fisherman or mariner haunting the seas, nor being in service with any kiddier or carrier of any corn grain or meal for provision of the city of London, nor with any husbandman in husbandry, nor in any city, town corporate or market town, in any of the arts or sciences limited or appointed by this statute to have or take apprentices, nor being retained by the year or half the year at the least, for the digging, seeking, finding, getting, melting, fining, working, trying, making of any silver, tin, lead, iron, copper, stone, sea coal, stone coal, moor coal, or charcoal, nor being occupied in or about the making of any glass, nor being a gentleman born, nor being a student or scholar in any of the universities or in any school, nor having lands, tenements, rents or hereditaments of the clear yearly value of forty shillings for term of life or of one estate of inheritance, nor being worth in goods and chattels to the value of ten pounds, nor having a father or mother then living, or other ancestor whose heir apparent he is, then having lands, tenements or hereditaments of the yearly value of X pounds or above, or goods or chattels of the value of XL pounds, nor being a necessary or convenient officer or servant lawfully retained as is aforesaid, nor having a convenient farm or holding whereupon he may or shall employ his labour, nor being otherwise lawfully retained according to the true meaning of this statute, shall after the foresaid last day of September now next ensuing by virtue of this statute, be compelled to be retained to serve in husbandry by the year, with any person that keepeth husbandry, and will require any such person so to serve within the same shire where he shall be so required.

5 Eliz. c. 4 (1563), *Statutes of the Realm*, iv, 415

6   Gentlemen and yeomen

Thomas Wilson, a government servant of modest means, the younger son of a
gentleman, here bitterly attributes the improved position of the yeomanry to
their having persuaded gentlemen to give them long leases. Many of these, he
says, were agreed on the eve of Henry VIII's debasement of the currency which,
in effect, reduced the *real* value of their rents, at the expense of the gentry. The
yeomen, therefore, benefits doubly from inflation: the rents in effect cost him
less than initially, while the prices of his agricultural products are rising because
of this very inflation. On the other hand, the gentry are losing doubly: through
the falling value of their rents and the higher cost of their extravagant living.
This explanation is, of course, over-simplified and exaggerated. Undoubtedly
some gentry adjusted themselves to the changed situation while others failed
hopelessly: but modern research has eroded the generalisations about the gentry
which were acceptable in the recent past.

The cause that hath made the yeomanry in England so great [in times
past] I cannot rightly call a policy, because it was no matter invented
and set down by authority for the bettering of that state of people, but
rather by the subtlety of them and simplicity of gentlemen; for the
yeomanry and mean people being servants and vassals to the gents, who
are the possessors and lord[s] of the lands and lordships and could not
occupy all their lands themselves but placed farmers therein at a time
when by reason of the great wars money was scarce and all things else
cheap, and so lands let at a small rent, the yeomen and farmers told the
gentlemen, their landlords, that they could not be at so great charges to
manure and inclose and improve their grounds, and repair and re-edify
their houses ruined by war unless they would let them the said land for
some time. And if they would so do, and at a smaller rent, they would
pay them some piece of money for a fine, and so much money yearly.
The gentlemen, improvident of what should come after, and glad to
have money in hands, did let unto the said farmers all their lands and
lordships (saving their dwelling) after the rate aforesaid, some for 30,
some 40 and some 50, some 200 years. Soon after, the king, by reason of
the want of money, altered the coin and caused that which was before
but 6d. to go for 12d. and after that again lessened it as much more, so
that he that was wont to pay but 3d. which though it were all one in
value yet hereby it came to pass that he which paid before 1 pound
weight in silver for his farm, paid now but a quarter, and the yeomen
at that time having most money, carrying it to the Mint, had for every
pound 4, paying for the minting, and the king besides got a great mass
of money by his said mint. This device, and then the price of corn,

cattle and all farmers' commodities increasing daily in price, and the gentleman who is generally inclined to great and vain expense had no more than would keep his house and some small rent, and therefore could not spend away prodigally much of the wealth of the land, because he hath no superfluity. And the baser sort, which by this means had got the wealth, had never the inclination to spend much. . . . But since these long leases are grown to expire the gentlemen by this begin to beware how to be so overreached.

> T. Wilson, 'The State of England, *anno. dom.*
> 1600', ed. F. J. Fisher, *Camden Misc.* xvi
> (1936), pp. 38–9

7 Poor tenants and rising rents

This extract, and the one which follows, provides a different account of rural life from that given by Wilson. Real poverty is depicted in the first, not simply falling living standards; and in the second, the lord is depicted as the oppressor of his tenants, not the victim of the yeomanry (as in II. 6 above). Harrison's account in the second passage of the condition of the copyholders is, like Wilson's of the gentry, too generalised to be accurate; but copyholders—descendants of the medieval villeins who had commuted their services into payment of cash and/or kind—were particularly vulnerable if their entry fines (premiums payable on succession to the land) had not been permanently fixed. Others were much more secure.

. . . the inhabitants of many places of our country are devoured and eaten up and their houses either altogether pulled down or suffered to decay by little and little, although sometime a poor man peradventure doth dwell in one of them, who, not being able to repair it, suffereth it to fall down and thereto thinketh himself very friendly dealt withal, if he may have an acre of ground assigned unto him whereon to keep a cow or wherein to set cabbages, radishes, parsnips, carrots, melons, pompons [pumpkins], or suchlike stuff, by which he and his poor household liveth as by their principal food, sith they can do no better. And as for wheaten bread, they eat it when they can reach unto the price of it, contenting themselves in the meantime with bread made of oats or barley: a poor estate, God wot!

> W. Harrison, *Description of England*, ed. F. J.
> Furnivall (1877), i, 258–9

... three things ... are grown to be very grievous unto them, to wit: the enhancing of rents ...; the daily oppression of copyholders, whose lords seek to bring their poor tenants almost into plain servitude and misery, daily devising new means and seeking up all the old how to cut them shorter and shorter, doubling, trebling and now and then seven times increasing their fines, driving them also for every trifle to lose and forfeit their tenures (by whom the greatest part of the realm doth stand and is maintained) to the end they may fleece them yet more, which is a lamentable hearing. The third thing they talk of is usury, a trade brought in by the Jews, now perfectly practised almost by every Christian and so commonly that he is accounted but for a fool that doth lend his money for nothing.

> W. Harrison, *Description of England*, ed. F. J.
> Furnivall (1877), i, 241–2

8 A deserted village, 1598

A poetic version of the above. (Notice the strong echoes of this verse in Oliver Goldsmith's *The Deserted Village* written nearly two centuries later.)

> I know where is a thief and long hath been,
> Which spoileth every place where he resorts:
> He steals away both subjects from the Queen,
> And men from his own country of all sorts.
> Houses by three, and seven, and ten he raseth,
> To make the common glebe his private land:
> Our country cities cruel he defaceth,
> The grass grows green where little Troy did stand,
> The forlorn father hanging down his head,
> His outcast company drawn up and down,
> The pining labourer doth beg his bread,
> The plowswain seeks his dinner from the town.
> O Prince, the wrong is thine, for understand,
> Many such robberies will undo thy land.

> Epigram of the Rev. Thomas Bastard, in
> *Tudor Economic Documents*, ed. R. H. Tawney
> and Eileen Power, iii, 80

9   Enclosure by agreement

It is important to bear in mind that the evidence of manorial conflict and exploitation is more dramatic, and therefore more widely quoted, than that for internal co-operation and agreement on the use of land. The following passage is an interesting example of voluntary enclosure resulting from agreement between the tenants and their lord in their mutual interests, with individual rights set out and safeguarded.

16th October 20 Elizabeth: . . . It is condescended and agreed at this court between Sir Edward Baynton, knight, lord of the manor aforesaid, and his tenants of the same, that they shall inclose and make several their lands in the common fields of Foxham and Avon, and also to exchange one with another for the same. And the said tenants that so doth exchange and inclose doth agree to pay yearly to the said Sir Edward and Dame Anne, now his wife, one bushel of beans for every yardland they have during the lives of the said Sir Edward and Dame Anne and either of them. . . .

2nd October 21 Elizabeth: . . . Item they present as follows, viz., It is ordered and agreed by the assent and consent of the lord of this manor and all the tenants of the same that no tenant shall put into the corn fields and mead at the breach thereof but two rother beasts or horse beasts for every acre, and they that have no land in the fields shall have no common there under penalty for each and every beast or horse put contrary to this order, Forfeit 10s.

And also it is ordered and agreed as follows, viz. That no tenant shall have going upon the lain sand fields but three sheep for every acre that he there hath, and two sheep for every acre that he hath in the fallow clay fields, and that none of the lord's tenants wanting sheep of his own to stuff his ground in the fields shall put out his common there to any other than to the lord's tenants, under penalty to each of them for each sheep, Forfeit 4d. . . .

> Bremhill Court Book, in E. Kerridge, *Agrarian Problems in the Sixteenth Century and After* (1969), p. 165

10   The export of grain

Here is interesting evidence of the possibility of extreme fluctuations in the harvest. Licences to export could be granted in areas where supplies were abundant, even though there might be scarcity elsewhere in England. The heavy cost of land transport acted as a severe barrier to internal distribution while water transport (in this case to Spain or Portugal) from a maritime county was relatively cheap. An additional reason for encouraging export was the shortage of salt in 'that country', i.e. county.

A letter to the commissioners for the restraint of grain and victuals within the county of Devon, signifying unto them that the Queen's Majesty, being informed of the great plenty of grain this year within that county of Devon, not only sufficient for the inhabitants but are able to spare a convenient quantity for others, is well pleased that William Curtis, citizen of London, should be licenced to transport three hundred quarters of wheat into Spain or Portugal, returning for the same so much salt, whereof that country hath some lack at this present. They are therefore required to give order that the said William Curtis, or the bringer hereof, may be served of the said proportion of wheat as conveniently may be without enhancing of the prices or troubling of the markets, taking heed that under colour hereof no greater number be transported than is appointed, for which cause it is thought convenient that they should appoint some trusty person to have care from time to time to such as shall have like licences; and so having taken bonds that within four months after the same wheat or any part thereof shall be transported he shall bring into the same county so much salt for the benefit thereof, to the intent that, paying the custom, he may be suffered to transport the said three hundred quarters accordingly.

A licence to export grain in time of plenty, 11 October 1579, *Tudor Economic Documents*, i, 161

11 The food shortage

This is a striking example of vigorous efforts by the Privy Council to ensure that corn, in time of great scarcity, should be distributed to those in need. But in this, as in most of the economic and social legislation, the implementation depended on the justices of the peace, who were often substantial landowners with special interests to protect. Notice the close control by licence over middlemen (badgers) as well as over bakers and brewers. Engrossers of corn are singled out for particular consideration; many of them may well have been engaged in cornering a scarce commodity for their own profit but some of them were performing the necessary services of a wholesaler.

You shall buy no corn to sell it again.

You shall neither buy nor sell any manner of corn but in the open market, unless the same be to poor handicraftsmen or day-labourers within the parish where you do dwell that cannot conveniently come to the market towns by reason of distance of the place, according to such direction as shall be given unto you in that behalf by the justices of the peace of that division within which you do dwell, or two of them, and to none of these above one bushel at a time. That the justices of the peace within their several divisions have special regard that engrossers of corn be carefully seen unto and severely punished according to the law, and where such are found, to make certificate thereof and of the proofs to the Queen's Majesty's attorney general for the time being, who is directed speedily to inform against them for the same, and to see also that none be permitted to buy any corn to sell again but by special licence.

That they take order with the common bakers for the baking of rye, barley, peas, and beans for the use of the poor, and that they appoint special and fit persons diligently to see their people well dealt withal by the common bakers and brewers in all towns and places in their weight and assize, and effectually to enquire for and search out the default therein, and thereupon to give order for punishment of the offenders severely according to the law, and where any notable offence shall be in the bakers, to cause the bread to be sold to the poorer sort under the ordinary prices in part of punishment of the baker.

That no badgers of corn, bakers or brewers do buy any grain, or covin or bargain for the same, but in the time of open market, and that but by licence under the hand of the justices of the division where they do dwell, or three of them, and that they weekly bring their licence with them to the market where they do either buy or sell, and that the licence contain how much grain of what kind and for what place they are licenced to buy and carry, that there be set down upon the licence the day, place, quantity and price the corn is bought at, that they take but measurably for the carriage, baking and brewing thereof, that they show their book weekly to such as the justice of the division wherein they dwell shall appoint, being no bakers or badgers of corn. And that those persons every 14 days make report to the justice of the division wherein they dwell how the people are dealt withal by the badgers, bakers and brewers. And that such as have otherwise sufficient to live on, or that are known to be of any crime or evil behaviour, be not permitted to be badgers of corn, nor any badgers to be permitted but such as the statute doth limit, and that none be permitted to buy or provide corn in the market in grass as badger and baker and such like,

upon pain of imprisonment, until one hour after the full market be
begun, that the poor may be first served.

> Orders devised by the special commandment
> of the Queen's Majesty for the relief and ease
> of the present dearth of grain within the realm,
> 1586, in *English Economic History, Select Docu-
> ments*, ed. Bland, Brown and Tawney, pp.
> 347–80

12 Famine

By the last decades of the sixteenth century the balance between corn and wool
production was being restored, and the anti-enclosure acts (primarily against
conversion to sheep rearing) had fallen into desuetude. In 1593 they were
repealed. The severe famine of 1594–7 led to a restoration of some of the
restraints, as set out in this extract from the Act of 1598. This was in essence a
panic measure. The true cause of the famine was not enclosure but three wet
summers. (Note that the measure applies to about half the counties of England,
the majority of them in the Midlands where the land was most easily convert-
ible from corn to sheep.)

Be it enacted . . . that whereas any lands or grounds at any time since
the seventeenth of November in the first year of her Majesty's reign
have been converted to sheep pastures or to the fattening or grazing of
cattle, the same lands having been tillable lands, fields or grounds such
as have been used in tillage or for tillage by the space of twelve years
together at the least next before such conversion, according to the
nature of the soil and course of husbandry used in that part of the
country, all such lands and grounds as aforesaid shall, before the first
day of May which shall be in the year of Our Lord God one thousand
five hundred and ninety nine, be restored to tillage, or laid for tillage in
such sort as the whole ground, according to the nature of that soil and
course of husbandry used in that part of the country, be within three
years at the least turned to tillage by the occupiers and possessors
thereof, and so shall be continued for ever.

> An Act for the maintenance of husbandry and
> tillage, 39 Eliz. c. 2 (1598), *Statutes of the Realm*,
> iv, 894

13 The search for industrial stability

These clauses from the Statute of Artificers form part of the attempt to maintain
a stable labour force by ensuring that appointments are for one year and
apprenticeships for seven. The weakening of the gild controls, and of the

corporate cities in which they were exercised, arose in part from the movement of industry out into rural districts or into unincorporated towns. In these conditions masters had been able to use unskilled labour for short or long periods to suit industrial needs rather than conform to rigid gild regulations. (See II. 15.) From the government's point of view the use of casual labour held the threat of political and social instability; to the gilds and their members these changing conditions presented the dangers of effective competition, since prices could be reduced where conditions and standards of labour were not enforced. In the interest of diversification and expansion, however, the decline of gild restraints was essential. (For a further extract from the statute see II. 5 above.)

Be it further enacted by the authority aforesaid that no manner of person or persons after the foresaid last day of September now next ensuing shall retain, hire or take in to service, or cause to be retained, hired or taken into service, nor any person shall be retained, hired or taken into service, by any means or colour, to work for any less time or term than for one whole year in any of the sciences, crafts, mysteries or arts of clothiers, woollen cloth weavers, tuckers, fullers, cloth-workers, shearmen, dyers, hosiers, tailors, shoemakers, tanners, pewterers, bakers, brewers, glovers, cutlers, smiths, farriers, curriers, saddlers, spurriers, turners, cappers, hatmakers or feltmakers, bowyers, fletchers, arrowhead-makers, butchers, cooks or millers.

. . . And be it further enacted . . . that after the first day of May next coming it shall not be lawful to any person or persons other than such as now do lawfully use or exercise any art, mystery or manual occupation, to set up, occupy, use or exercise any craft, mystery or occupation now used or occupied within the realm of England or Wales, except he shall have been brought up therein seven years at the least as apprentice. . . .

> An Act touching the divers orders for artificers, labourers, servants of husbandry and apprentices, 5 Eliz. c. 4, *Statutes of the Realm*, pp. 415, 420

14 Proposal to strengthen industrial control

Here, some fourteen years after the Statute of Artificers, we have in this pamphlet strong conservative arguments in favour of the traditional control of industry. The Act 5 Edward VI, c. 6, referred to in the text, was the Act for the Making of Woollen Cloth of 1552, which established close control over cloth production and gave the power of supervision to the corporate towns and their officials.

One thing more I have remembered, and in my heart I do wish it, that the clothiers might be urged to dwell in towns, which in continuance of time would much beautify the realm, and thereby make towns more populous, as it was meant by the Act of 5 E. 6; in which towns good order might be taken for repressing of all falsehood used by the clothier or workman; whereby also the order of Flanders for searching and sealing might be easily brought to pass, viz. the weaver to present his cloth woven before the masters of his company, and there to be proved, the fuller or clothworker likewise, and the dyer for his part also; which being found perfect every of them might set to their seals particularly, with a confirmation of the town seal where it was made. And if it be faulty in any point material, then the seals wherein the offence is shall want, and thereby give knowledge to the buyer; and if the offence be great, then permit not to seal at all.

Leake's Treatise on the Cloth Industry, 1577,
Tudor Economic Documents, iii, 224–5

15   Some London wage rates

The following document provides a selection of the numerous occupations essential to a sixteenth-century capital. Note that the second highest wage-rate is that of the dyer, an important worker in the cloth finishing trade which some industrialists were anxious to develop further to compete with the high quality work of the Flanders dyers. Brewing, the best paid employment in this list—more than twice as much as some—perhaps sheds light on contemporary tastes.

To the best and most skilful workmen, journeymen and hired servants of any of the companies hereunder named:

Clothworkers by the year with meat and drink £5
Fullers by the year with meat and drink £5
Shearmen by the year with meat and drink £5
Dyers by the year with meat and drink £6 13s. 4d.
Tailors hosier by the year with meat and drink £4
Drapers being hosiers by the year with meat and drink £4
Shoemakers by the year with meat and drink £4
Pewterers by the year with meat and drink £3 6s. 8d.
Whitebakers by the year with meat and drink £4 13s. 4d.
Brewers by the year with meat and drink £10
The underbrewer by the year with meat and drink £6
The foredrayman by the year with meat and drink £6
The miller by the year with meat and drink £6

The other drayman by the year with meat and drink £3 6s. 8d.

The tunman by the year with meat and drink £3 6s. 8d.

Alebrewers by the year with meat and drink £6, by the day with meat and drink 8d.

Saddlers by the year with meat and drink £4

Turners by the year with meat and drink £4 6s. 8d.

Cutlers by the year with meat and drink £4 6s. 8d.

Blacksmiths by the year with meat and drink £6

Curriers by the year with meat and drink £6

Bowyers by the year with meat and drink £4

Fletchers by the year with meat and drink £4

Brownbakers by the year with meat and drink £3 6s. 8d.

Farriers by the year with meat and drink £4

Glovers by the year with meat and drink £3 6s. 8d.

Cappers by the year with meat and drink £4 13s. 4d.

Hatmakers and feltmakers by the year with meat and drink £4 13s. 4d.

Butchers by the year with meat and drink £6

Cooks by the year with meat and drink £6

> Some London wage rates, 1588, in *Proclamations*, ed. Hughes and Larkin, iii, 22–3

16 Textile production

This Act forms part of the attempt to encourage the textile finishing industry in this country. While England was dependent on Antwerp for her principal outlet no significant growth of the English finishing industry was likely, since the Netherlands was a great centre for finishing textiles. With the decline of Antwerp and the diversification of English trade from the late-sixteenth century, this side of the English textile industry grew in importance.

For the better employment and relief of great multitudes of the Queen's Majesty's subjects, using the art and labour of cloth-working, it may please the Queen's most excellent Majesty, at the most humble suit of her said subjects, that it be enacted, and be it enacted by the authority of this present parliament, that from henceforth for every nine cloths unwrought, hereafter to be shipped or carried into any the parts beyond the seas, contrary to the form of any statute heretofore made and now remaining in strength, by force of any licence hereafter to be granted, the party that shall ship or carry over the same, shall ship and carry over also one like woollen cloth of like sort, length, breadth and goodness, ready wrought and dressed; that is to say, rowed, barbed, first coursed and shorn from the one end to the other, so that every tenth cloth passing over the seas in form aforesaid may and shall be dressed within this realm, before the same shall be shipped or transported over, upon pain to forfeit for every such nine cloths so to be shipped or transported contrary to the meaning of this act, ten pounds. . . .

> An Act touching cloth-workers and cloths
> ready wrought to be shipped over the sea,
> 8 Eliz. c. 6 (1566), *Statutes of the Realm*, iv, 489.

17 Relief work

The Act of 1576 formed an important part of the developing poor law legislation which culminated in the consolidated Poor Law Act of 1598, made permanent in 1601. This clause was an enlightened attempt to use poor law provisions to rehabilitate the unemployed by setting them to work on the parish stock of raw materials. It could only be alleviatory: during the time of a major industrial slump there would be a surplus of these products and they could be unsaleable. This measure also included severe conditions for the unsettled vagabond—though he might have started his wandering because of a genuine desire to seek work wherever it could be found. The basic weaknesses of the poor law system as it was evolving were lack of both skilled administrative staff and local funds.

. . . To the intent youth may be accustomed and brought up in labour and work, and then not like to grow to be idle rogues, and to the intent also that such as be already grown up in idleness and so rogues at this present may not have any just excuse in saying that they cannot get any service or work and then without any favour or toleration worthy to be executed, and that other poor and needy persons being willing to work may be set on work, be it ordained and enacted by the authority aforesaid that in every city and town corporate within this realm a competent store and stock of wool, hemp, flax, iron or other stuff by the appointment and order of the mayor, bailiffs, justices or other head officers having rule in the said cities or towns corporate (of themselves and all others the inhabitants within their several authorities to be taxed, levied and gathered) shall be provided. And that likewise in every other market town or other place within every county of this realm where (to the justices of peace or greater part of them in their general sessions yearly next after Easter within every limit shall be thought most meet and convenient) a like competent store and stock of wool, hemp, flax, iron or other stuff as the country is most meet for, by appointment and order of the said justices of peace or the greater part of them in their said general sessions (of all the inhabitants within their several authorities to be taxed, levied and gathered) shall be provided, the said stores and stocks in such cities and towns corporate to be committed to the hands and custody of such persons as shall, by the mayor, bailiffs, justices or other head officers having authority in every such city or town corporate, be appointed, and in other towns and places to such persons as to the said justices of peace or the greater part of them in their said general sessions of the peace in their several counties shall be by them appointed.

> An Act for the setting of the poor on work, and
> for the avoiding of idleness, 18 Eliz. c. 3,
> *Statutes of the Realm*, iv, 611

18   Coal cutting on a small scale

In a famous work, *The Rise of the British Coal Industry*, Professor J. U. Nef drew attention to the expansion of coal production, more especially in the north-eastern coalfield, and the beginnings of large scale production between 1560 and 1640. The general picture is now regarded as somewhat over-drawn but certainly important beginnings were made. The following extract is concerned with a very small mine at Sheffield. The pickmen worked at the coal face, the barrower was responsible for collecting the coal and bringing it from the seam, the bankman brought it to the surface by means of a pulley and stacked the coal in banks.

```
From the iiiith of October unto the xith of
              the same                        v days
Coals got in hard quarters xlv
   cont. in loads xv                      xxxs ⎫
Coals got in small quarters xlv                ⎬ xlvs
   cont. in loads xv                       xvs ⎭
                                              inde

Paid to the pickman           viis. vid.
Item to the barrower          iis. vid.  ⎫
Item to the bankman           iiis. ixd. ⎬ xvs. viiid.
Item Candles to the barrower     viiid. ⎭
Item Candles to the pickman       xvd.
                                          and
```

So remains clear with xd. got in the Endgate . . . xxxs. [sic]

> B.M. Add. MS. 27532, f. 85, cited in L.
> Stone, 'An Elizabethan Coalmine', *Ec. Hist.
> Rev.*, 2nd series, iii, 105

19   Infringement of a patent

The following report by a commission of enquiry concerns the complaints of an industrialist, William Humphrey (of the Mineral and Battery Works), that his patent for lead smelting had been infringed. The defence offered is that these methods have been in use in Derbyshire for about a generation and there is evidence to support this view. Humphrey himself, who did pioneer work in developing smelting techniques, died in 1579 but the case dragged on into 1584 when it lapsed.

On Tuesday being 8 August 1581 we met in a market town called Bakewell and from thence, for the better execution of the commission, we went and surveyed the lead mill or melting house at Beauchief there lately erected by virtue of Her Majesty's privilege by William Humfrey for the working and melting of lead ore and making of lead. Which contains 2 furnaces and 2 pair of bellows in the same house. Which bellows are blown by water. Which house is still continued working by virtue of the said privilege by Nicholas Strelley esq.

And the next day we did also repair to a place in the Peak at Calver used likewise for the melting and working of lead ore and making of lead. Which house, we were informed, belongs to Paul Tracy esq. And found his men at work upon the lead ore. And upon view and survey of the same at work we perceived that the house and 2 furnaces and 2 pair of bellows as well as the workmanship, melting of the ore and making of lead, were made and wrought in the same order and manner as at Beauchief without any apparent difference, saving only the bellows at Calver are blown by men's feet and without water. And this workhouse at Calver seems to be very lately builded and it was informed to us, the Commissioners, to be builded, used and wrought and still continued contrary to the said privilege and without the consent of the same.

Moreover, we the commissioners were informed that divers other melting houses in like manner are used and builded in the country contrary to the privilege. Which we did not view because they were dispersed in sundry parts and that the depositions did sufficiently prove the same. Furthermore we understood only of two houses, besides that at Beauchief, are used by authority of the privilege. Whereof one is used by Sir John Zouch, Kt. and the other by Mr. Wendesley of Wendesley. And that the rest which, by common report, are 10 or 12 are without consent of the privilege as now plainly appears by the depositions.

Report of Commissioners on lead working, 1581, cited in M. B. Donald, *Elizabethan Monopolies* (1961), pp. 158–9

20   The outcry over monopolies

This is an excerpt from the heated debate over monopolies which developed in the parliament of 1601. There had been earlier vigorous complaints about monopolies but the Queen's promises of redress had not been fulfilled. Wroth's list stretches over a very wide area of industrial and domestic commodities; and the highly independent barrister, William Hakewill, took the opportunity of warning his hearers that bread might one day be in the list. This interjection was, of course, ironical; but it underlined the constitutional implications of the whole debate. Those who thought like him were now arguing, against the advice of the crown ministers, that this prerogative matter should be brought within the framework of parliament, a view entirely unacceptable to the Queen. The following is part of a speech made by Sir Robert Wroth:

There have been divers patents granted since the last parliament. These are now in being, viz. the patents for currants, iron, powder, cards, horns, ox shin-bones, train oil, lists of cloth, ashes, bottles, glasses, bags, shreds of gloves, aniseed, vinegar, sea-coals, steel, aquavitae, brushes, pots, salt, saltpetre, lead, accedence, oil, transportation of leather, calamine stone, oil of blubber, fumothoes, or dried pilchards in the smoke, and divers others.

Upon reading of the patents aforesaid, Mr. Hackwell of Lincoln's Inn stood up and asked this: 'Is not bread there?'

'Bread,' quoth another.

'This voice seems strange,' quoth a third.

'No,' quoth Mr. Hackwell, 'but if order be not taken for these, bread will be there before the next parliament.'

Heywood Townshend, *Historical Collections* (1680), pp. 238–9

21   Some of the things we bought

The following are a few examples from a lengthy list of imports, followed by their official valuation. The import duty charged was usually 5 per cent. The values are those of 1558 which remained unchanged until the issue of a new book of rates in 1604.

Abces [i.e. A.B.Cs or spelling books] the gross
    containing xii dozen in paper   iiis.

Alasicratrina [a herb used in the treatment of
    venereal disease] the pound   iiis. iiid.

Apples called pippins or rennets the bushell   xiid.

Balls called tennis balls the thousand   xxs.

Bears living, the bear   xxs.

Cloth of silver wrought the yard   xls.

Daggers fine for children the dozen   iis.

Ear pickers of bone the gross   vs.

Feather beds old or new the piece   xiiis. iiiid.

Ginger the pound   xviiid.

Hose of silk knit the pair   xxvis. viiid.

Nux vomica [a source of strychnine] the pound   vid.

Shirts of mail, the piece   xxvis. viiid.

Virginals single the pair   xvis. viiid.

Selected from *A Tudor Book of Rates*, ed.
T. S. Willan (Manchester, 1962)

22 The control of imports

This measure reflects the anxiety over the adverse trade balance and the un-employment in England during the depression, and sets forth the contemporary mercantilist doctrines about industrial self-sufficiency.

Whereas heretofore the artificers of this realm of England as well within the city of London as within other cities, towns and boroughs of the same realm, that is to wit, girdlers, cutlers, saddlers, glovers, point-makers, and such like handicraftsmen, have been in their said faculties greatly wrought, and greatly set on work, as well for the sustentation of themselves, their wives and families, as for a good education of a great part of youth of this realm in good art and laudable exercise, besides the manifold benefits, that by means or by reason of their knowledges, inventions, and continual travail, daily and universally came to the whole estate of the commonwealth of this said realm.

Yet notwithstanding, so now it is, that by reason of the abundance of foreign wares brought into this realm from the parts of beyond the seas, the said artificers are not only less occupied, and thereby utterly impoverished, the youth not trained in the said sciences and exercises, and thereby the said faculties, and the exquisite knowledges

thereof, like in short time within this realm to decay; but also divers
cities and towns within this realm of England much thereby impaired,
the whole realm greatly endamaged, and other countries notably
enriched, and the people thereof well set on work, to their commodities
and livings, in the arts and sciences aforesaid, and to the great discourage of the skilful workmen of this realm, being in very deed
nothing inferior to any stranger in the faculties aforesaid.

For reformation whereof be it enacted by our Sovereign Lady the
Queen's Highness, and by the Lords Spiritual and Temporal, and by
the Commons of this present parliament assembled and by the authority
of the same, that no person or persons whatsoever, from or after the
feast of the nativity of St. John Baptist now next ensuing, shall bring
or cause to be brought into this realm of England from the parts of
beyond the seas any girdles, harness for girdles, rapiers, daggers, knives,
hilts, pommels, lockets, chapes, dagger-blades, handles, scabbards,
and sheaths for knives, saddles, horse-harness, stirrups, bits, gloves,
points, leather-laces or pins, being ready made or wrought in any parts
of beyond the seas, to be sold, bartered or exchanged within this realm
of England or Wales; upon pain to forfeit all such wares so to be
brought contrary to the true meaning of this act, in whose hands
soever they or any of them shall be found, or the very value thereof.

> An Act for the avoiding of divers foreign
> wares made by handicraftsmen beyond the
> seas, 5 Eliz. c. 7 (1563), *Statutes of the Realm*, iv,
> 428

23   Opposition to free trade

The decline of Antwerp, and the difficulties of competing effectively on the
European market against continental producers, contributed to an intensifica-
tion of the conflict between the Merchant Adventurers and the interlopers (i.e.
private traders). Here the Adventurers put forward the familiar argument that
the interlopers' indiscriminate rush to sell their goods all over Germany and
Italy, as against their own practice of concentrating their supplies at Middleburgh and Emden (previously at Antwerp), put these private merchants at the
mercy of local interests who either offer low prices or poor quality exports in
return. These and other arguments in the petition are, in fact, loaded in favour
of the Adventurers, whose traditionalist, monopolistic methods and organisation of trade became increasingly inappropriate to the expansionist trading
conditions of the seventeenth century.

Reasons exhibited by the Merchant Adventurers touching their trade

Experience of many years continuance hath proved their ordered and governed trade not only in and to divers places of the Low Countries, but also in and to Germany, as lately at Hamburg and presently at Emden and at Middleburgh in Zeeland, to be and always to have been to the great benefit of this commonwealth, as well in uttering great quantity of woollen cloths and other merchandises as in advancing and maintaining good prices and reputation of the same. . . .

For now, whilst the Merchant Adventurers keep their trade at Middleburgh and Emden, divers English subjects carry cloths to Hamburg, and landing the same there carry the same afterwards within the land to divers other cities of Germany and Italy; and having once brought their cloths so far into the land, the people, knowing they can not carry them back again without extreme loss, do either offer very low prices there for or else offer, for the same, evil silks or other deceitful wares in barter, whereof grow to our country all the losses aforesaid. And also thereby such wanderers into the land bring the hatred of all the merchants of the inland cities upon our countrymen, noting us of such covetousness as that we can not be contented with the trade from our own country to their ports, but also that we will have the trade from them within the land; where, if we left them the one they would well agree and like that we should have the other. . . .

Also, divers English subjects do continually ship cloths and other merchandises from hence to Calais, Gravelines, Dunkirk and Newport, and so keep a continual traffic with those of Flanders and other places under the government of the Prince of Parma, to their great wealth and maintenance, and withal do carry to them much victual of all kinds, without which they could hardly maintain their state. And thereby the traffic at Middleburgh is greatly hindered, etc.

Wherefore, the said Merchants Adventurers humbly pray that according to their lordships' former decree all English subjects may be prohibited to ship any merchandises to any port of Germany between the rivers of Ems and the Skaw, and that no subject aforesaid or other do ship any merchandise of victual from hence to Calais, Gravelines, Dunkirk or Newport or elsewhere to the hurt of the said trade at Middleburgh or Emden.

Petition from the Merchant Adventurers to the Privy Council to suppress interlopers, ?1584, *Tudor Economic Documents*, ii, 66–7

24 Criticism of the Merchant Adventurers

This excerpt from a report by a parliamentary committee is hostile to the Merchant Adventurers and is a summary of some of the arguments against them, expressed in a discussion a year after the Queen's death. The strength of the Adventurers and their supporters seems to have been no more than 40 out of a total of some 400 Members of Parliament.

The committees from the House of the Commons sat five whole afternoons upon these bills; there was a great concourse of clothiers and merchants, of all parts of the realm, and especially of London; who were so divided, as that all the clothiers, and, in effect, all the merchants of England, complained grievously of the engrossing and restraint of trade by the rich merchants of London, as being to the undoing or great hindrance of all the rest; and of London merchants three parts joined in the same complaint against a fourth part; and of that fourth part some standing stiffly for their own company yet repined at other companies. Divers writings and informations were exhibited on both parts; learned counsel was heard for the bill and divers of the principal aldermen of London against it; all reasons exactly weighed and examined; the bill, together with the reasons on both sides, was returned and reported by the committees to the House where, at the third reading, it was three several days debated, and in the end passed with great consent and applause of the House (as being for the exceeding benefit of all the land) scarce forty voices dissenting from it.

Wealth—The increase of the wealth generally of all the land by the ready vent of all the commodities to the merchants at higher rate; for where many buyers are, ware grows dearer; and they that buy dear at home must sell dear abroad. This also will make our people more industrious.

Equal distribution—The more equal distribution of the wealth of the land, which is a great stability and strength to the realm, even as the equal distributing of the nourishment in a man's body; the contrary whereof is inconvenient in all estates and oftentimes breaks out into mischief when too much fullness doth puff up some by presumption and too much emptiness leaves the rest in perpetual discontent, the mother of desire of innovations and troubles: and this is the proper fruit of monopolies. Example may be in London and the rest of the realm. The custom and impost of London come to a hundred and ten thousand pound a year, and of the rest of the whole realm but to seventeen thousand pound.

Strength—The increase of shipping, and especially of mariners, in all ports in England. How greatly the mariners of the realm have decayed in all places, of latter times, and with how great danger of the state in these late wars, is known to them who have been employed in that kind of service; who do also attribute the cause thereof to this restraint of trade, free traffic being the breeder and maintainer of ships and mariners, as by memorable example in the Low Countries may be seen.

Profit of the Crown—The increase of custom and subsidy to the King which doth necessarily follow the increase of foreign traffic and wealth. . . .

> Instructions touching the bill for free trade,
> 1604, *Journals of the House of Commons*, i, 218

25 Interest legalised again, 1571

In rehearsing the recent legal history of the right to take interest, this statute is a reflection of the changing climate of opinion. The Act of 1545 which (like that of 1571) permitted the taking of interest up to 10 per cent is here praised as a measure by which the vice of usury was well repressed—the word usury having here its modern meaning of excessive interest, not simply interest. The Edwardian Act of 1552, part of the extreme Protestant reaction, prohibited the taking of all interest, and so gave rise, as in medieval conditions, to bogus transactions which, while masking the interest, in fact led to excessive charges—'to the great undoing of many gentlemen, merchants, occupiers [of land] and other'. The legalisation of interest was essential for encouraging increased investment in industry and trade.

Whereas in the parliament holden the seven and thirty year of the reign of our late Sovereign Lord King Henry the Eighth of famous memory there was then made and established one good Act for the reformation of usury, by which Act the vice of usury was well repressed, and specially the corrupt chevisance and bargaining by way of sale of wares and shifts of interest; and where since that time by one other Act made in the fifth and sixth years of the reign of our late Sovereign Lord King Edward the Sixth the said former Act was repealed, and new provisoes for repressing of usury devised and enacted, which latter Act hath not done so much good as was hoped it should, but rather the said vice of usury, and specially by way of sale of wares and shift of interest, hath much more exceedingly abounded, to the utter undoing of many gentlemen, merchants, occupiers and other, and to the importable hurt of the commonwealth, as well for that in the said

latter Act there is no provision against such corrupt shifts and sales
of wares, as also for that there is no difference of pain, forfeiture or
punishment upon the greater or lesser exactions and oppressions by
reason of loans upon usury: Be it therefore enacted that the said
latter statute, made in the fifth and sixth years of the reign of King
Edward the Sixth, and every branch and article of the same, from and
after the five and twenty day of June next coming, shall be utterly
abrogated, repealed and made void; and that the said Act, made
in the said seven and thirty year of King Henry the Eighth, from and
after the said five and twenty day of June next coming, shall be revived
and stand in full force, strength and effect.

And be it further enacted that all bonds, contracts and assurances,
collateral or other, to be made for payment of any principal or money
to be lent, or covenant to be performed upon, or for any usury in
lending or doing of anything against the said Act now revived,
upon or by which loan or doing there shall be reserved or taken
above the rate of ten pounds for the hundred for one year shall be
utterly void.

> An Act against usury, 13 Eliz. c. 8 (1571),
> *Statutes of the Realm*, iv, 542

26   Interest and usury: the survival of an ancient doctrine, 1595

The medieval view of interest is here lucidly presented—more than twenty
years after the passage of the Act legalising it. To Miles Mosse, a clerical pamphleteer, usury differs from interest, not in the amount charged but in whether
loss has been sustained by the lender or not: only if loss *has* been sustained is
interest legitimate. Hence he puts forward the primitive view that, if the
borrower returns the loan on the day promised, no interest is due. On such a
basis Tudor commerce could never have expanded.

Note by the way, for the better discovery of the userer's evil
dealing, that howsoever he, to gloss with the world, is wont to con-
found the names of interest and usury—and men are wont to say that
they take interest and lend upon interest when indeed they take
usury and lend upon usury—yet that there are two manifest and essential differences between usury and interest, which do so distinguish
the one from the other, as they cannot possibly be confounded. One
difference is this: usury is an overplus or gain taken more than was
lent; interest is never gain or overplus above the principal but a

recompence demanded and due for the damage that is taken, or the gain that is hindered through lending. Another difference is this: usury accrueth and groweth due by lending from the day of borrowing unto the appointed time of payment; interest is never due but from the appointed day of payment forward and for so long as I forbear my goods after the day in which I did covenant to receive them again. So that, if once I have lent freely unto a certain day, I shall not demand interest for any damage sustained or gain hindered, during that term of time for which I have lent unto another. But if at the covenanted time I receive not mine own again, then what harm soever do betide me after that day for the forbearing thereof, reason will that it be recompensed of the borrower. And so much of interest, and of the difference between it and usury.

Miles Mosse, *Arraignment and Conviction of Usury*, 1595, *Tudor Economic Docs.*, iii, 378–9

27 An insurance policy of a Bristol merchant

This insurance policy is drawn from a series of model business documents collected by a Bristol merchant and meant as a handbook for his young colleagues. The insurance cover, given here, is extensive, from acts of war to '. . . all other perils, losses and misfortunes', at a charge of 7 per cent of the value. The liability is spread among three insurers.

In the name of God Amen. Be it known unto all men by these presents: that Thomas Aldsworth, merchant of the city of Bristol, doth make assurance and causeth himself to be assured from the port of the said city of Bristol, called Hungroad, unto the port of Lisbon in the Kingdom of Portugal, and therehence directly back again to the aforesaid port of Bristol: upon the body, tackle, apparel, ordinance, munition, artillery, boat, and other furniture, of the good ship called the Gabriel of Bristol, of the burden of 60 tons, or thereabouts. And also upon all goods, wares, and merchandises laden or to be laden in the aforesaid ship the Gabriel, whereof is master under God for this present voyage R.M. or by what other name the master of the ship may or shall be called. Beginning the adventure from the day and hour of the lading of the anchor, spreading the sail, and departure of the said ship from Hungroad aforesaid. And so shall continue and endure until such time as the said ship with all her said furniture, and all the goods and merchandises laden in her, shall return and safely arrive back again from Lisbon unto the port of Hungroad aforesaid, and there hath surged and moored at an anchor by the space of 24 hours in good safety. Touching the adventures and perils which we the assurers hereafter named are contented to bear and take upon us this present voyage, are of the seas, men of war, fire, enemies, pirates, rovers, thieves, jettisons, letters of mark and countermark, arrests, restraints, and detainments of Kings and Princes and of all other persons, barratry of the master and mariners, and of all other perils, losses, and misfortunes whatsoever they be, or howsoever to the damage or hurt of the said ship and goods or any part or parcel thereof. And that in case of any misfortunes: it shall then be lawful to the assured, his factor, servant, or assignee, to sue, labour, and travail, for, in and about, the defence, safeguard and recovery of the said ship and goods, and all other the premises, without any prejudice to this assurance. To the charges whereof, we the assurers shall contribute each one according to the rate and quantity of his sum herein assured. It is to be understood that this present writing and assurance shall be of as much force, strength and effect, as the best and most surest policy or writing of assurance which hath been ever heretofore used to be made in Lombard Street, or now within the Royal Exchange in London. And so we the assurers are contented, and do promise and bind ourselves and every of us, our heirs, executors and assignees for the true performance of the premises, according to the use and custom of the said Street, or Royal Exchange. Confessing ourselves to be fully satisfied and paid of and for the considerations due us after the rate of 7. upon the 100. And in testimony of the truth, we the assurers have hereunto severally subscribed our names and sums of money assured, given in London the 19 day of September, 1589.

I, W.N. merchant of London am content with this assurance   25*li*
(which God preserve) for 25 pounds this 19 day of
September, 1589.

I, R.T. merchant of London am content with this assurance   25*li*
(which God preserve) for 25 pounds this 20 day of
September, 1589.

I, M.R. merchant of Bristol am content with this assurance 25 *li* [*Sic.*]
(which God preserve) for 15 pounds this 21 day of
September, 1589.

'I. B. Marchant', *The Marchants Avizo* (1589),
ed. P. McGrath (1957), pp. 52–3

III

INTELLECTUAL DEVELOPMENTS

1 How to get on in the world

The eminent Elizabethan statesman, William Cecil, Lord Burghley, wrote tracts giving advice to his sons; and these tracts circulated in manuscript. The following are two extracts from them, the first to his elder son, Thomas, the other to his younger son, Robert. The advice to Thomas was given on the eve of his departure for France; but the proposal for a devout study of the bible each day, though badly needed, seems to have had little effect: Thomas stole cash in the possession of his tutor and seduced a high-born French lady, sometimes said to be a nun. His father despised him and gave him no encouragement towards political advancement. The younger son, Robert, the recipient of the second piece of advice, was the apple of his father's eye and rose to the highest offices in the state. Reading these passages, it is easy to see why Burghley is widely regarded as the original of Polonius.

(i)

And after this private prayer every morning, whereunto you must bind yourself and for no matter of business leave it undone, you shall make you ready in your apparel in cleanly sort, doing that for civility and health and not for pride. This done, then shall you at your appointed hour resort to such common prayer as shall be accorded to be said by you and your company, and my meaning is that you shall use the manner of the prayer of the Church of England in Latin. And for your instructions you shall do well to get some small commentary of the Psalter, and after your prayer to peruse the exposition of all dark and hard speeches for which purpose you may procure Hominius; you shall also do the like in procuring some shorter exposition of the words of the New Testament and the Old, daily perusing the hard places. And for commodity of carriage you shall do well to procure these books to be bound in parchment and to note the same books with your pen in such sort as at your return I may see how you have observed this precept. You may understand that in one whole year you may read over the Psalter twelve times so that you cannot but come to the understanding thereof. And as for the New Testament, you shall read it over four times in the year; the Old Testament you shall by order read over once in the year. This is all the study I mean you shall bestow in divinity, saving you shall do well to be present with attention [at] every sermon that you may hear being preached by men of such judgment as accordeth with your profession here.

Also, you shall before you go to sleep every night upon your knees reverently and devoutly ask forgiveness of your offences, calling them curiously and exactly from the morning through every hour of the day until that time to your remembrance, and not only to remember them but to consider by what occasion you fell unto them, to be sorry for them, to detest them, to make an appointment to avoid the occasions the next day, to beseech Almighty God to guide you in the next day by His Holy Spirit that you fall not into the like. If you offend in forgetting of God by leaving your ordinary prayers or suchlike, if you offend in any surfeiting by eating or drinking too much, if you offend any other ways by attending and minding any lewd and filthy tales or enticements of lightness or wantoness of body, you must at evening bring both your thoughts and deeds as you put off your garments, to lay down and cast away those and all suchlike that by the devil are devised to overwhelm your soul and so to burden it by daily laying on filth after filth that when you would be delivered thereof you shall find the burden thereof too weighty. And so, ending this matter, I commend you to the tuition of the Almighty God, having in this behalf discharged myself of the care committed to me by God, being your earthly and corruptible father, remitting you again by education of you from childhood to this state wherein you are and from ignorance to knowledge to the hands of God from whom I received you as His gift, and if you shall please Him and serve Him in fear, I shall take comfort of you; otherwise I shall take you as no blessing of God but a burden of grief and decay of my age.

A memorial for Thomas Cecil, Advice to a Son,
ed. L. B. Wright, Folger Shakespeare Library
(Ithaca, 1962), pp. 4-5

(ii)

When it shall please God to bring thee to man's estate use great providence and circumspection in the choice of thy wife, for from thence may spring all thy future good or ill; and it is an action like a stratagem in war where man can err but once. If thy estate be good, match near home and at leisure; if weak, then far off and quickly. Inquire diligently of her disposition and how her parents have been inclined in their youth. Let her not be poor how generous soever, for a man can buy nothing in the market with gentility. Neither choose a base and uncomely creature altogether for wealth, for it will cause contempt in others and loathing in thee. Make not choice of a dwarf or a fool, for from the one thou mayest beget a race of pygmies, the other may be thy daily disgrace; for it will irk thee to have her talk, for then thou shalt find to thy great grief that there is nothing more fulsome than a she-fool. Touching the government of thy house, let thy hospitality be moderate and according to the measure of thine own estate, rather plentiful than sparing—but not too costly— for I never knew any grow poor by keeping an orderly table. But some consume themselves through secret vices and their hospitality must bear the blame. Banish swinish drunkards out of thy house, which is a vice that impairs health, consumes much, and makes no show, for I never knew any praise ascribed to a drunkard but the well-bearing of drink, which is a better commendation for a brewer's horse or a drayman than for either gentleman or servingman. Beware that thou spend not above three of the four parts of thy revenue, nor above one-third part of that in thine house, for the other two parts will do no more than defray thy extraordinaries, which will always surmount thy ordinaries by much. For otherwise shalt thou live like a rich beggar in a continual want, and the needy man can never live happily nor contented, for then every least disaster makes him ready either to mortgage or to sell, and that gentleman which then sells an acre of land loses an ounce of credit, for gentility is nothing but ancient riches. So that if the foundations sink, the building must needs consequently fail.

Certain Precepts for the well ordering of a
man's life, Advice to a Son, pp. 9–10

(iii)

... There—my blessing with thee!
And these few precepts in thy memory
Look thou character. Give thy thoughts no tongue,
Nor any unproportion'd thought his act.
Be thou familiar, but by no means vulgar.
Those friends thou hast, and their adoption tried,
Grapple them to thy soul with hoops of steel;

But do not dull thy palm with entertainment
Of each new-hatch'd, unfledg'd courage. Beware
Of entrance to a quarrel; but, being in,
Bear't that th'opposed may beware of thee.
Give every man thy ear, but few thy voice;
Take each man's censure, but reserve thy judgment.
Costly thy habit as thy purse can buy,
But not express'd in fancy; rich, not gaudy;
For the apparel oft proclaims the man;
And they in France of the best rank and station
Are of a most select and generous choice in that.
Neither a borrower nor a lender be;
For loan oft loses both itself and friend,
And borrowing dulls the edge of husbandry.
This above all—to thine own self be true,
And it must follow, as the night the day,
Thou canst not then be false to any man. . . .

Hamlet, I, 3

2   Early morning at school

The following are extracts from the statutes of 1560 for Westminster School, re-founded after the Reformation. The sections cited set out the qualifications and duties of the masters and the general purpose of education; as well as give an insight into the conditions of life at the school, and indicate the work done between 6 a.m. and 9 a.m. The rest of the day is spent in the study of the classics and the biblical texts, and two hours of the week are to be devoted to music. The day ends at 7.30 p.m.

There shall be two masters, one of whom shall be called Head Master. The one shall be a master of grammar or of arts, the other a bachelor of arts at least, if this can conveniently be done. All the scholars shall be under their government, both of them shall be religious, learned, honourable and painstaking, so that they may make their pupils pious, learned, gentlemanly and industrious. The Dean of Christ Church, Oxford, and the Master of Trinity College, Cambridge, shall in turn elect these masters, with the consent of the Dean of Westminster. Their duty shall be not only to teach Latin, Greek and Hebrew Grammar, and the humanities, poets and orators, and diligently to examine in them, but also to build up and correct the boys' conduct, to see that they behave themselves properly in church, school, hall and chamber, as well as in all walks and games, that their faces and hands are washed, their heads combed, their hair and nails cut, their clothes both linen and woollen, gowns, stockings and shoes kept clean, neat, and like a gentleman's, and so that lice or other dirt may not infect or offend themselves or their companions, and that they never go out of the college precincts without leave. They shall further appoint various monitors from the gravest scholars to oversee and note the behaviour of the rest everywhere and prevent anything improper or dirty being done. If any monitor commits an offence or neglects to perform his duty he shall be severely flogged as an example to others. . . .

The Teaching and Ordering of the Scholars

All the scholars shall spend the night in one or two chambers, two in a bed.

At 5 o'clock that one of the Monitors of Chamber (who shall be four in number) who shall be in course for that week, shall intone 'Get up.' They shall immediately all get up and, kneeling down, say Morning Prayers, which each shall begin in turn, and all the rest follow, in alternate verses, saying, 'O Lord, holy father, almighty, everlasting God,' as in Chapter 10 On Divine worship.

Prayers finished they shall make their beds. Then each shall take any dust or dirt there may be under his bed into the middle of the chamber, which, after being placed in various parts of the chamber, shall then be swept up into a heap by four boys, appointed by the Monitor, and carried out.

Then two and two in a long line they shall all go down to wash their hands; when they come back from washing they shall go into school and each take his place.

Prayers to be said in School

At 6 o'clock the Master shall come in and, kneeling at the top of the school, begin the following prayers, the boys following in alternate verses. [Ps. 67 and responses after.]

Prayers finished, the Master shall go down to the First or lowest class and hear a part of speech and of a verb in its turn. He shall pass on from the First class to the Second, from the Second to the Third, from the Third, if he thinks fit, to the Fourth, which sits in his part of the school till 7 o'clock, to examine if any obscurity arises.

Meanwhile one of the Prefects of School goes to the head of each form in the Head Master's as well as in the Usher's part, and gets from them in writing the names of those absent from morning prayers and hands them to the Usher. Another Prefect (who always performs this duty by himself) carefully inspects each boy's hands and face, to see if they have come with unwashed hands to school, and when the Head Master comes in immediately presents them to him. This order shall be kept every day.

At 7 o'clock the Fourth Form shall transfer itself from the Usher's part to the Head Master's. He shall come into school, and all the heads of each form shall after 7 o'clock hand him the names of their absents. And one of the Prefects of School shall hand the names of those who were absent from school after 6 and 7 o'clock in the evening on the day before to the Head Master and Usher respectively. Then all the classes shall say by heart what has been read to them in this order; viz. the Custos shall always begin and shall carefully observe the rest saying it afterwards.

At 8 o'clock the Head Master shall set some sentence to the Fourth Class to translate, to the Fifth to vary, and to the Sixth and Seventh to turn into verse. The Custos shall take it from his lips and translate it first. The Usher too shall set some sentence to the Third and Second Form to translate, and to the First also, but for them it shall be very short.

The vulguses shown up by each shall be written on the same morning, and next day they shall say it in order by heart, before or about 9 o'clock. The Custos of each of the upper forms shall first say by heart the lesson of the form next to him and explain it. Then the Head Master shall read the same lesson to his boys as the Usher to his.

> Statutes of Westminster School, 1560, trans. A. F. Leach in *Educational Charters and Documents* 598–1909 (Cambridge, 1911), pp. 497–509

3   The hardships of a public school education?

Roger Ascham, tutor to Elizabeth I when she was in her teens, and her Latin Secretary after her accession, here tells us the circumstances in which he came to write his famous book, *The Schoolmaster*. The discussion took place one afternoon in 1563, while the Court was at Windsor; and the Master Secretary is William Cecil (later Lord Burghley), secretary of state. After the conversation, printed below, one of the courtiers, Sir Richard Sackville, asked Ascham to put his ideas on education into writing. This led to *The Schoolmaster*, almost complete when Ascham died in 1568 and published in 1570. It set out the basis of good education: a firm grounding in the classics and the development of character, all accomplished by sympathy and patience, not by harsh discipline.

'I have strange news brought me,' saith Master Secretary, 'this morning, that divers scholars of Eton be run away from the school for fear of beating.' Whereupon Master Secretary took occasion to wish that some more discretion were in many schoolmasters in using correction than commonly there is, who many times punish rather the weakness of nature than the fault of the scholar. Whereby many scholars that might else prove well be driven to hate learning before they know what learning meaneth, and so are made willing to forsake their book and be glad to be put to any other kind of living.

Master Petre, as one somewhat severe of nature, said plainly that the rod only was the sword that must keep the school in obedience and the scholar in good order. Master Wotton, a man mild of nature, with soft voice and few words, inclined to Master Secretary's judgment and said, 'In mine opinion, the schoolhouse should be indeed, as it is called by name, the house of play and pleasure, and not of fear and bondage. And as I do remember, so saith Socrates in one place of Plato. And therefore if a rod carry the fear of a sword, it is no marvel if those that be fearful of nature choose rather to forsake the play than to stand always within the fear of a sword in a fond man's handling.' Master Mason, after his manner, was very merry with both parties, pleasantly playing both with the shrewd touches of many curst boys and with the small discretion of many lewd schoolmasters. Master Haddon was fully of Master Petre's opinion and said that the best schoolmaster of our time was the greatest beater, and named the person. 'Though,' quoth I, 'it was his good fortune to send from his school unto the university one of the best scholars indeed of all our time, yet wise men do think that that came so to pass rather by the great towardness of the scholar than by the great beating of the master. And whether this be true or no, you yourself are best witness.' I said somewhat farther in the matter, how and why young children were sooner allured by love than driven by beating to attain a good learning—wherein I was the bolder to say my mind because Master Secretary courteously provoked me thereunto, or else, in such a company, and namely in his presence, my wont is to be more willing to use mine ears than to occupy my tongue.

R. Ascham, *The Schoolmaster* (1570), ed. L. V. Ryan, Folger Shakespeare Library (1967), pp. 6–7

4 The need for schools

In his oration to the Commons on election as Speaker, Thomas Williams warns his listeners of the dangers of ignorance through lack of schools. Parsons had in many cases served as local schoolmasters but, Williams argues, covetousness has taken much from the Church and sufficient good livings are no longer available. In the event, as Professor W. K. Jordan has shown (*Philanthropy in England, 1480–1660*), from around this time onwards there were very considerable endowments by wealthy men, as well as municipal foundations, for new grammar schools. A generation after Williams's speech Harrison was writing of the progress already made. See (ii) below.

(i) . . . for how now be all schools, benefices and other like rooms furnished, and yet those for schools so few that I dare say a hundred schools want in England, which before this time have been. And if in every school there had been but an hundred scholars, yet that had been ten thousand. So that now I doubt whether there be so many learned men in England as the number wants of these scholars.

> Speaker Williams, House of Commons, January 1563, D'Ewes, *The Journals of all the Parliaments during the reign of Queen Elizabeth* (1682), pp. 64–5

(ii) Besides these universities also there are great number of grammar schools throughout the realm, and those very liberally endued for the better relief of poor scholars, so that there are not many corporate towns now under the Queen's dominion that hath not one grammar school at the least, with a sufficient living for a master and usher appointed to the same.

> William Harrison, *Description of England*, ed. F. J. Furnivall (1877), p. 83

5 The classics in peril?

Richard Mulcaster, first headmaster of Merchant Taylor's School and later High Master of St. Paul's, attempted in his *Positions* . . . (1581) to broaden the educational curriculum for the gentry and diminish the dominance of classical studies.

It is no proof because Plato praiseth it, because Aristotle alloweth it, because Cicero commends it, because Quintilian is acquainted with it, or any other else . . . that therefore it is for us to use.

Richard Mulcaster, Positions, cited in Joan
Simon, Education and Society in Tudor England
(Cambridge, 1966), p. 353

6 The universities

Harrison here reflects the contemporary expansion of the universities and the pressure of the gentry to gain places for their sons there. These developments form part of a fundamental change in English universities in the century after the Reformation: their secularisation and their growth to meet the social and cultural demands of the gentry as well as the needs of the professions and the government service.

In my time there are three noble universities in England to wit, one at Oxford, the second at Cambridge, and the third in London; of which the first two are the most famous, I mean Cambridge and Oxford, for that in them the use of the tongues, philosophy, and the liberal sciences, besides the profound studies of the civil law, physic, and theology, are daily taught and had; whereas in the latter the laws of the realm are only read and learned, by such as give their minds unto the knowledge of the same. In the first there are not only divers goodly houses builded foursquare, for the most part of hard freestone or brick, with great numbers of lodgings and chambers in the same for students after a sumptuous sort, through the exceeding liberality of kings, queens, bishops, noblemen, and ladies of the land, but also large livings and great revenues bestowed upon them (the like whereof is not to be seen in any other region, as Peter Martyr did oft affirm), to the maintenance only of such convenient numbers of poor men's sons as the several stipends bestowed upon the said houses are able to support. . . .

. . . In most of our colleges there are also great numbers of students, of which many are found by the revenues of the houses and other by the purveyances and help of their rich friends, whereby in some one college you shall have two hundred scholars, in others an hundred and fifty, in divers, a hundred and forty, and in the rest less numbers, as the capacity of the said houses is able to receive; so that at this present, of one sort and other, there are about three thousand students nourished in them both (as by the late survey it manifestly appeared). They were erected by their founders at the first only for poor men's sons, whose parents were not able to bring them up unto learning, but now they have the least benefit of them, by reason the rich do so encroach upon them. And so far hath this inconvenience spread itself that it is in my time an hard matter for a poor man's child to come by a fellowship (though he be never so good a scholar and worthy of that room). Such packing also is used at elections that not he which best deserveth, but he that hath most friends, though he be the worst scholar, is always surest to speed, which will turn in the end to the overthrow of learning.

Harrison, *Description of England*, ed. F. J. Furnivall (1877), pp. 70–71, 76–7

7   The Inns of Court

Like the universities, the Inns attracted increasing numbers from the middle classes, though many students stayed only a year or two to pick up a smattering of law, sufficient to be of use to them on a bench of magistrates. The more serious student stayed several years, sometimes after a period of one or two years at one of the universities. In his *Elizabethan House of Commons*, Sir John Neale has shown the increasing number of graduates and members of Inns who were elected to parliament. We print also a celebrated account of other aspects of life at the Inns. Highly coloured though it is it conveys some of the other attractions of this form of education.

(i)

To these two [universities] also we may in like sort add the third, which is at London (serving only for such as study the laws of the realm), where there are sundry famous houses, of which three are called by the name of Inns of the Court, the rest of the Chancery, and all builded beforetime for the furtherance and commodity of such as apply their minds to our common laws. Out of these also come many scholars of great fame, whereof the most part have heretofore been brought up in one of the aforesaid universities and prove such commonly as, in process of time, rise up (only through their profound skill) to great honour in the commonwealth of England. They have also degrees of learning among themselves and rules of discipline, under which they live most civilly in their houses, albeit that the younger sort of them abroad in the streets are scarce able to be bridled by any good order at all. Certes this error was wont also greatly to reign in Cambridge and Oxford between the students and the burgesses, but as it is well left in these two places, so in foreign countries it cannot yet be suppressed.

Harrison, *Description of England*, ed. F. J. Furnivall (1877), pp. 82–3

(ii)

Shallow: . . . I dare say my cousin William is become a good scholar; he is at Oxford still, is he not?

Silence: Indeed, sir, to my cost.

Shal.: 'A must, then, to the Inns o' Court shortly. I was once of Clement's Inn; where I think they will talk of mad Shallow yet.

Sil.: You were call'd 'lusty Shallow' then, cousin.

Shal.: By the mass, I was call'd anything; and I would have done anything indeed too, and roundly too. There was I, and little John Doit of Staffordshire, and black George Barnes, and Francis Pickbone, and Will Squele a Cotsole man—you had not four such swinge-bucklers in all the Inns o' Court again. And I may say to you we knew where the bona-robas were, and had the best of them all at commandment. Then was Jack Falstaff, now Sir John, a boy, and page to Thomas Mowbray, Duke of Norfolk.

Sil.: This Sir John, cousin, that comes hither anon about soldiers?

Shal.: The same Sir John, the very same. I see him break Scoggin's head at the court gate, when 'a was a crack not thus high; and the very same day did I fight with one Sampson Stockfish, a fruiterer, behind Gray's Inn. Jesu, Jesu, the mad days that I have spent! and to see how many of my old acquaintance are dead!

King Henry the Fourth, II, 3, 1

8   What's gone wrong with our schools and universities?

The famous early seventeenth-century poem, *The Lie*, attributed to Sir Walter Raleigh, comments savagely on contemporary society. The following are two stanzas in which the poet attacks both the pedantry and the superficiality of contemporary education.

> Tell wit how much it wrangles
> In tickle points of niceness.
> Tell wisdom she entangles
> Herself in over-wiseness.
> And when they do reply
> Straight give them both the lie. . . .

Tell arts they have no soundness,
But vary by esteeming.
Tell schools they want profoundness
And stand too much on seeming.
If arts and schools reply,
Give arts and schools the lie.

W. Raleigh, *The Lie*

9   A retrospect: radicalism at the universities

Thomas Hobbes, looking back over the events of his lifetime, sees among the origins of the English civil wars, the rise of a critical spirit among the men who have come down from the universities. He presents his case in the form of a dialogue and here draws attention to the alliance between Presbyterian clergy and radical members of parliament. The belief in 'popular' government, that is government resting on popular support, like the democracy to be studied in the classics, represents to Hobbes the undermining of the established order of stable monarchical rule. Hence he sees 'the core of the rebellion' as lying in the education received at the universities.

B: But how came the people to be so corrupted? and what kind of people were they that did so seduce them? . . .

A: There were an exceeding great number of men of the better sort, that had been so educated as that in their youth having read the books written by famous men of the ancient Grecian and Roman commonwealths concerning their polity and great actions, in which books the *popular* government was extolled by the glorious name of liberty and monarchy disgraced by the name of tyranny, they became thereby in love with their forms of government. And out of these men were chosen the greatest part of the House of Commons; or, if they were not the greatest part, yet, by advantage of their eloquence, they were always able to sway the rest. . . .

B: I know indeed that, in the beginning of the late war, the power of the Presbyterians was so very great that not only the citizens of London were, almost all of them, at their devotion, but also the greatest part of all other cities and market towns of England. But you have not yet told me 'by what art and what degrees they became so strong'.

A: It was not their art alone that did it; but they had the concurrence of a great many gentlemen that did no less desire a popular government in the civil state than these ministers did in the church. And as these did in the pulpit draw the people to their opinions and to a dislike of the church government, canons and common prayer book, so did the others make them in love with democracy by their harangues in the Parliament and by their discourses and communication with people in the country, continually extolling of liberty and inveighing against tyranny, leaving the people to collect of themselves that this tyranny was the present government of the state. And as the Presbyterians brought with them into their churches their divinity from the universities, so did many of the gentlemen bring their politics from thence into the Parliament. But neither of them did this very boldly in the time of Queen Elizabeth. And though it be not likely that all of them did it out of malice, but many of them out of error, yet certainly the chief leaders were ambitious ministers and ambitious gentlemen, the ministers envying the authority of bishops, whom they thought less learned, and the gentlemen envying the Privy Council, whom they thought less wise than themselves. For 'tis a hard matter for men who do all think highly of their own wits (when they have also acquired the learning of the university) to be persuaded that they want any ability requisite for the government of a commonwealth. . . .

The core of rebellion (as you have seen by this and read of other rebellions) is in the universities which, nevertheless, are not to be cast away, but to be better disciplined. That is to say, that the politics there taught be made to be, as true politics should be, such as are fit to make men know that it is their duty to obey all laws whatsoever that shall, by the authority of the king, be enacted, till, by the same authority, they shall be repealed.

> T. Hobbes, 'Behemoth', c. 1668, in *Select Tracts Relating to the Civil Wars in England*, ed. F. Maseres (1815), pp. 459, 477–8, 511

10   A suitor to a patron

The Elizabethan nobility, and other leading men of the time, exercised considerable influence in their recommendations of candidates for public office. But their patronage extended also throughout the range of contemporary culture, including painting, literature, the theatre and the Church. Outstanding among these patrons was Robert Dudley, Earl of Leicester, whose influence is fully discussed in Dr. Eleanor Rosenberg's book, *Leicester, Patron of Letters*. Here is a characteristic request for support from a translator.

. . . [Desiring], as the common custom is, some patron that might both bring authority to this my little book, and also, if need should be, defend it from the bitter taunts of envious tongues, I have not espied, right honourable, any one, either for his bountiful goodness towards my friends (which commonly men respect) or else for his favourable and gracious humanity toward scholars (in whose number I am) unto whom I might so justly give this small cumbrous trifle and especial token of good will as to your lordship, whose honourable goodness or rather magnificence, both your honour's nursery of learning [i.e. Oxford University], and as I can boldly say, the University of Cambridge, with my poor friends, have most abundantly tasted of. . . .

> Dedication by T. Nunce of a translation of *Octavia*, published in 1566, to the Earl of Leicester, cited in E. Rosenberg, *Leicester, Patron of Letters* (New York, 1955), p. 159

11   A book of homilies for the Earl of Bedford

In submitting his translation of a book of homilies to the Earl of Bedford, the author, John Bridges, Vicar of Herne, sets out the general reasons for dedications and then gives his own. The word 'exhibition' as used by him here means a maintenance grant. The opinion he quotes on Machiavelli was typical of that held by most Elizabethans. St. Paul's Cross, outside the Cathedral, was a popular place for sermons, sometimes—but not always—government inspired.

Sundry men have sundry meanings in dedicating their studies and travails to such men of honour as you are. Some seek their friendship and goodwill, some augmentation of living, some authority to commend and set forth their works and labour, some one thing, some another. I have herein been led with none of these considerations. For your Honour's benevolence and friendship I long sithence well found and proved, which gave me the best part of that exhibition whereby I lived in Italy three or four years together, and whereby also I live at this day the better. I mean the experience and knowledge which I learned in that space. . . . Mine only intent in this simple labour of mine was to show myself some manner of ways not unmindful of your Lordship's liberality so long agone bestowed upon me, nor of that great humanity which the same used about a nine years past, twice in one Lent at the Court being then in White Hall, toward so poor a man as I, preventing my bashful nature and slackness of speech toward my superiors, with such courteous affability, that among the manifold experiences which I had eftsoons before seen in you of a noble and gentle nature, I judged this not one of the least. . . . And for proof that I never forgot your Honour's goodwill and friendship, I could show you the three books of Machiavelle's discourses translated by me out of Italian into English, more than fourteen years past, which I thought to have presented unto your Honour but was stayed therefrom, partly because I heard the work inveighed against at Paul's Cross, as a treatise unworthy to come abroad into men's hands, and partly for that I hoped still to have some other matter more plausible and acceptable to give unto the same.

> Dedication of Bridges's translation of R. Walther, *An Hundred, three score and fiftene Homelyes . . .* (1572), in H. S. Bennett, *English Books* and *Readers, 1558–1603* (Cambridge, 1965), pp. 33–4

12   A patron renders an account of his patronage

The Puritan preacher Thomas Wood, carrying his religious egalitarianism into practice, was accustomed to write in the frankest of terms to the most eminent of his contemporaries. The Earl of Leicester, among others, was the object of his stern criticism for his failure to support the godly. It is interesting that this leading courtier takes the trouble to send a full reply to Wood. (See also Document **IV. 19.**)

. . . look of all the bishops that can be supposed that I have commended to that dignity since my credit any way served, and look whether they were not men as well thought of as any among the clergy before. Look of all the deans that in that time also have been commended by me. Look into the University of Oxford likewise, whereof I am Chancellor, and see what heads of houses be there now in comparison of those I found. And do but indifferently examine how the ministry is advanced there, even where were not long ago not only many ill heads but as many the worst and untoward scholars for religion. Beside this, who in England hath had, or hath, more learned chaplains belonging to him than I, or hath preferred more to the furtherance of the church of learned preachers.

> Earl of Leicester to Thomas Wood, 19 August 1576, in *Letters to Thomas Wood, Puritan, 1566–1567*, ed. Patrick Collinson (Bulletin of the Institute of Historical Research, Special Supplement, No. 5, 1960), p. 13

13   The torments of Court life

These two extracts from poems by Edmund Spenser reflect the tensions and bitterness of suitors for patronage. The poet must have seen these conditions from close quarters having been a member of the households of the Earl of Leicester and of Lord Grey de Wilton. The 'aged' tree in the first of these poems refers to Lord Burghley, Elizabeth's minister for forty years. The Earl of Essex another of Spenser's patrons, was a bitter contestant for the power enjoyed by Burghley and his son, Robert Cecil.

(i)

O grief of griefs, O gall of all good hearts,
To see that virtue should despised be
Of him that first was raised for virtuous parts,
And now, broad spreading like an aged tree,
Lets none shoot up that nigh him planted be.

> Spenser, *The Ruins of Time*, in *The Poetical Works of Edmund Spenser*, ed. J. C. Smith and E. de Selincourt (1932), p. 476

(ii)

Full little knowest thou that hast not tried
What Hell it is, in suing long to bide;
To lose good days that might be better spent;
To waste long nights in pensive discontent;
To speed today, to be put back tomorrow;
To feed on hope, to pine with fear and sorrow;
To have thy Prince's grace, yet want her Peer's;
To have thy asking, yet wait many years;
To fret thy soul with crosses and with cares;
To eat thy heart through comfortless despairs;
To fawn, to crouch, to wait, to ride, to run,
To spend, to give, to want, to be undone.

> Spenser, *Mother Hubbard's Tale*, *op. cit.*, p. 504

14   Are patrons necessary?

Bacon was a victim of the patronage system, in his case in politics, where, during the long dominance of the Cecils, his close relations, he could make little progress. Here, however, he makes a general observation about literary patronage.

Neither is the modern dedication of books and writings, as to patrons, to be commended: for that books (such as are worthy the name of books) ought to have no patrons but truth and reason.

Bacon, *The Advancement of Learning*

15 Francis Bacon on reading

The following is an excerpt from his essay, *Of Studies*. In his lifetime there were three editions of his *Essays*: the first, containing ten essays, appeared in 1597 (a version of *Of Studies* was included); the second, in 1612, containing thirty-eight; and the third in 1625 containing fifty-eight. In the process the essays themselves were generally revised and enlarged.

Read not to contradict and confute; nor to believe and take for granted; nor to find talk and discourse; but to weigh and consider. Some books are to be tasted, others to be swallowed, and some few to be chewed and digested: that is, some books are to be read only in parts; others to be read, but not curiously; and some few to be read wholly, and with diligence and attention. Some books also may be read by deputy, and extracts made of them by others; but that would be only in the less important arguments and the meaner sort of books; else distilled books are like common distilled waters, flashy things. Reading maketh a full man; conference a ready man; and writing an exact man. And therefore, if a man write little, he had need have a great memory; if he confer little, he had need have a present wit; and if he read little, he had need have much cunning, to seem to know that he doth not. Histories make men wise; poets, witty; the mathematics, subtle; natural philosophy, deep; moral, grave; logic and rhetoric, able to contend.

Bacon, Essay, *Of Studies*

16 Restraints on freedom of thought

The invention of printing—the first time in history that society was faced with the problem of a mass medium—made the governments of Europe increasingly aware of a threat to their power. For now it was possible for dissenting opinion, whether political or religious, to be much more widely disseminated than hitherto. Hence the extensive use of censorship. In Elizabeth's reign, the Injunctions of 1559 set up a licensing system for books. In 1586 the detailed system of control of printing was set forth in a decree made in the Star Chamber. Excerpts from this document are given below. This kind of control should be borne in mind when considering the views of some historians that the Tudor period was a time of liberty and government by consent.

ITEM. That no printer of books, nor any other person or persons whatsoever, shall set up, keep or maintain any press or presses, or any other instrument or instruments for imprinting of books, ballads, charts, portraitures or any other thing or things whatsoever, but only in the City of London, or the suburbs thereof, and except one press in the University of Cambridge, and another press in the University of Oxford, and no more. And that no person shall hereafter erect, set up or maintain in any secret or obscure corner or place any such press or instrument, before expressed, but that the same shall be in such open place or places, in his or their house, or houses, as the Wardens of the said Company of the Stationers for the time being, or such other person or persons as by the said Wardens shall be thereunto appointed, may from time to time have ready access unto, to search for and view the same. . . .

ITEM. That no printer, nor other person or persons whatsoever, that have set up any press or instrument for imprinting within six months last past, shall hereafter use or occupy the same, nor any person or persons shall hereafter erect or set up any press or other instrument of printing till the excessive multitude of printers having presses already set up be abated, diminished and by death giving over, or otherwise brought to so small a number of masters or owners of printing presses, being of ability and good behaviour, as the Archbishop of Canterbury and Bishop of London for the time being shall thereupon think requisite and convenient for the good service of the realm, to have some more presses or instruments for printing erected and set up. . . .

ITEM. That no person or persons shall imprint or cause to be imprinted, or suffer by any means to his knowledge his press, letters or other instruments to be occupied in printing of any book, work, copy, matter or thing whatsoever, except the same book, work, copy, matter, or any other thing hath been heretofore allowed, or hereafter shall be allowed before the imprinting thereof, according to the order appointed by the Queen's Majesty's Injunctions, and been first seen and perused by the Archbishop of Canterbury and Bishop of London for the time being, or any one of them.

Star Chamber decree on printing, 1586, A.
Arber, *Transcript of Registers of Company of Stationers of London* (1875), ii, 808-10

17 Censorship in action

Here is a comment on the consequences of the Injunctions and the Star Chamber decree. Stubbes was a Puritan pamphleteer.

I cannot but lament the corruption of our time for (alas) now-a-days it is grown to be a hard matter to get a good book licensed without staying, peradventure, a quarter of a year for it; yea, sometimes two or three years before he can have it allowed, and in the end happly rejected too. So that that which many a good man hath . . . travailed long in . . . shall . . . never see the light, whilst . . . other books, full of all filthiness, scurrility, bawdry, dissoluteness, cosinage, conycatching and the like . . . are either quickly licensed or at least easily tolerated.

Philip Stubbes, *A Motive to Good Workes*, 1593, cited in *Shakespeare's England* (1917), ii, 222

18 William Camden on his methods as historian

In these extracts from his introduction to his *History of the reign of Queen Elizabeth*, Camden shows the remarkable advances made in the study of history since the end of the middle ages. It has moved far from chronicle and laudatory biography and involves the critical use of a whole range of documentary and other sources from official records to private interviews. In Camden the study of history is thereby enlarged. His work is marked also by a large measure of objectivity, though not quite so complete as he implies. He shows, too, his conservative approach, in one sense, in that he sets limits to the historian's enquiry into the secret origins of government action. His book was written in Latin to make it accessible to European scholars. Our passages are taken from the 1688 translation.

About eighteen years since, William Cecil, Baron of Burghley, Lord High Treasurer of England (when full little I thought of any such business) imparted to me, first his own, and then the queen's rolls, memorials and records, willing me to compile from thence an historical account of the first beginnings of the reign of Queen Elizabeth, with what intent I know not unless, while he had a desire to eternize the memory of that renowned queen, he would first see an introduction thereinto by my pains in this kind. I obeyed him, and not unwillingly, lest I might seem either to neglect the memory of that most excellent princess, or to fail his expectation and (which I prized as dear as them both) the truth itself. For in these papers, if anywhere, I had confident hopes to meet the real truth of passages lodged, as it were, in so many repositories.

But at my very first entrance upon the task, an intricate difficulty did, in a manner, wholly discourage me. For I lighted upon great piles and heaps of papers and writings of all sorts, reasonably well digested indeed in respect of the times, but in regard of the variety of the arguments very much confused. In searching and turning over whereof, whilst I laboured till I sweat again, covered all over with dust, to gather fit matter together (which I diligently sought for but more rarely found than I expected) that noble lord died, and my industry began to flag and wax cold in the business. Not long after, that incomparable princess also rendered her celestial soul to God. . . .

[Having failed to find someone else to take on the task] I buckled myself afresh to my intermitted study, and plied it harder than before. I procured all the helps I possibly could for writing it. Charters and grants of kings and great personages, letters, consultations in the council chamber, ambassadors' instructions and epistles, I carefully turned over and over. The parliamentary diaries, acts and statutes I thoroughly perused and read over every edict or proclamation. . . .

Mine own cabinets and writings I also searched into: who, though I have been a studious regarder and admirer of venerable antiquity, yet have I not been altogether careless of later and more modern occurrences but have myself seen and observed many things, and received others from credible persons that have been before me, men who have been present at the transacting of matters, and such as have been addicted to the parties on both sides in this contrariety of religion. All which I have in the balance of mine own judgement (such as it is) weighed and examined, lest I should at any time through a beguiling credulity incline to that which is false. For the love of truth, as it hath been the only incitement to me to undertake this work, so hath it also been my only scope and aim in it. Which truth to take from history is nothing else but, as it were, to pluck out the eyes of the beautifullest creature in the world and, instead of wholesome liquor, to offer a draught of poison to the readers' minds. . . .

. . . The hope of any gain hath not drawn me aside. To set the dignity of history to sale, to me (who have been ever well contented with a mean estate) always seemed base and servile. Suspicion of either affection or disaffection can here have no place. For of all those I am to mention I know scarce one by whom I have received any benefit or advantage, not one from whom I have received any injury: so as no man can reckon me amongst those that are either obnoxious or malicious. Such as are living I have said but little of, either in their praise or dispraise. By inveighing against the enemies of my country, to aim at the commendation of a good commonwealths man, and at the same time get the repute of a bad historian, I held a thing ridiculous. This I have been careful of, that, according as Polybius directeth, I might have an eye to the truth only. Neither shall any man (I trust) find lacking in me that ingenuous freedom of speech joined with modesty which becometh an historian. That licentiousness, accompanied with malignity and backbiting, which is cloaked under the counterfeit show of freedom, and is everywhere entertained with a plausible acceptance, I do from my heart detest. Things manifest and evident I have not concealed. Things doubtful I have interpreted favourably. Things secret and abstruse I have not pried into. 'The hidden meanings of princes,' saith that great master of history, 'and what they secretly design to search out, it is unlawful, it is doubtful and dangerous. Pursue not therefore the search thereof.' And, with Halicarnasseus, I am angry with those curious, inquisitive people who will needs seek to know more than by the laws is permitted them. . . .

Circumstances I have in no wise omitted, that not only the events of affairs, but also the reasons and causes thereof, might be understood. That of Polybius I like well: 'Take away from history why, how and to what end things have been done, and whether the thing done hath succeeded according to reason, and all that remains will rather be an idle sport and foolery, than a profitable instruction. And though for the present it may delight, for the future it cannot profit.

William Camden, *Annales* . . . (English translation, 1688), Introduction

19   An antiquarian on his life's work

In the work of John Stow we have another aspect of the diversification of Tudor culture. Stow lacked the education and scholarship of Camden but none of his enthusiasm. A London tailor—and not a very prosperous one at that—he devoted his life to elucidating the antiquity of his beloved native city. His *Survey of London*, worthy to rank with the work of other great Tudor antiquaries and topographers such as John Leland and William Lambarde, carries the reader from street to street in the City, furnishing him the whole time with an immense variety of fascinating historical detail. Our excerpt comes from the dedication to the Lord Mayor of London, the Commonalty and its citizens.

. . . I have attempted the discovery of London, my native soil and country, at the desire and persuasion of some my good friends, as well because I have seen sundry antiquities myself touching that place, as also for that through search of records to other purposes, divers written helps are come to my hands, which few others have fortuned to meet withall. It is a service that most agreeth with my professed travails. It is a duty that I willingly owe to my native mother and country, and an office that of right I hold myself bound in love to bestow upon the politic body and members of the same. What London hath been of ancient time men may here see, as what it is now every man doth behold. I know that the argument, being of the chief and principal city of the land, required the pen of some excellent artisan, but fearing that none would attempt and finish it, as few have assayed any, I chose rather (amongst other my labours) to handle it after my plain manner than to leave it unperformed. . . .

> John Stow, *A Survey of London*, *1603*, ed.
> C. L. Kingsford (Oxford, 1908), i, xcvii–
> xcviii

20 A sceptical view of historians

In spite of the considerable developments in historical study in the sixteenth century, and the wide interest aroused, to some the historian remained arrogant and pedantic. The following passage illustrates that even a great poet like Sidney could still be insensitive about another branch of literature.

The historian scarcely giveth leisure to the moralist to say so much, but that he, loaden with old mouse-eaten records, authorising himself (for the most part) upon other histories, whose greatest authorities are built upon the notable foundation of hearsay; having much ado to accord differing writers and to pick truth out of partiality; better acquainted with a thousand years ago than with the present age, and yet better knowing how this world goeth than how his own wit runneth; curious for antiquities and inquisitive of novelties; a wonder to young folks and a tyrant in table talk, denieth, in a great chafe, that any man for teaching of virtue, and virtuous actions, is comparable to him.

> Sir Philip Sidney, *An Apology for Poetry*, ed.
> G. Shepherd (1967), p. 105

21 The entertainment of the Queen

The Court patronage of the arts was extensive. Here, from payments out of the Chamber, we have grants for theatrical entertainments provided by groups of players who are supported by noblemen, as well as by a famous group of children attached to the royal chapel, and by a party of tumblers (acrobats). The Master of the Game, that is to say, of the bears and mastiffs, is also paid here for a show presented during the Christmas festivities. The refinement of the Elizabethan Court managed to find room for the squalid exercise of bear-baiting. The shillings and pence in the payments arise because the 'mark' (13s. 4d.) was a common unit of account.

1579–1580

To the Lord Straunge his tumblers upon a warrant signed by her Majesty's Privy Council dated at Whitehall 25th January 1579, in consideration of certain feats of tumbling by them done before Her Majesty upon Tuesday the 15th of the same month, the sum [of] £6. 13s. 4d., and more by way of Her Majesty's reward, 66s. 8d., in all £10

To Richard Farrant, Master of the Children of Her Majesty's Chapel, in consideration of one play by them presented before Her Majesty upon St. John's Day last past, the sum of £6. 13s. 4d., and more by way of reward, 66s. 8d., as by a warrant signed by Her Majesty's Privy Council, dated at Whitehall, 25th January 1579 doth appear £10

To the Lord Chamberlain's players upon the Council's warrant dated at Whitehall, 25th February 1579, in consideration of a play by them presented before Her Majesty upon St. Stephen's Day last past, £6. 13s. 4d., and more by way of reward, 66s. 8d., in all £10

. . . .

To the players of the Earl of Warwick upon the Council's warrant dated at Whitehall, 25th January 1579, in consideration of one play presented before Her Majesty on New Year's Day last £6. 13s. 4d., and more in reward by Her Majesty, 66s. 8d., in all £10

To the players of the Lord of Leicester upon the Council's warrant dated at Whitehall, 25th January 1579, for presenting of a play before Her Majesty on twelfth day last past, £6. 13s. 4d., and more by way of Her Majesty's reward, 66s. 8d., in all £10

To Thomas Bowes, esquire, Master of Her Majesty's Game at Paris Garden, upon the Council's warrant, dated at Whitehall 18th February 1579, for conveying the said game to the Court at Whitehall, in

Christmas holidays last past, and showing the same before Her Highness, and for his attendance   100s

.   .   .   .

*Dramatic Records in the Declared Accounts of the
Treasurer of the Chamber, 1558–1642*, ed. D.
Cook and F. P. Wilson (Malone Society,
Collections Vol. VI, 1961–2), pp. 16–17

22   A playwright on the plays

In his introduction to the published version of his play, *The Roaring Girl*,
thought to have been written jointly with Dekker, Thomas Middleton comments on the changing character of the theatre.

The fashion of play-making I can properly compare to nothing so
naturally as the alteration in apparel. For, in the time of the great
crop-doublet, your huge bombasted plays, quilted with mighty words
to lean purpose, was only then in fashion. And as the doublet fell,
neater inventions began to set up. Now in the time of spruceness,
our plays follow the niceness of our garments: single plots, quaint
conceits, lecherous jests, dressed up in hanging sleeves, and those are
fit for the times and the tearmers. Such a kind of light-colour summer
stuff, mingled with diverse colours, you shall find this published
comedy, good to keep you in an afternoon from dice at home in your
chambers. And for venery you shall find enough for sixpence, but well
couched and [i.e. if] you mark it. For Venus, being a woman, passes
through the play in doublet and breeches, a brave disguise and a safe
one, if the statute untie not her codpiece point.

   The book I make no question but is fit for many of your companies,
as well as the person itself, and may be allowed both gallery room at
the playhouse and chamber room at your lodging. Worse things,
I must needs confess, the world has taxed her for than has been written
of her. But 'tis the excellency of a writer to leave things better than he
finds 'em though some obscene fellow (that cares not what he writes
against others yet keeps a mystical bawdy-house himself, and entertains
drunkards to make use of their pockets and rent his private bottle-ale
at midnight) though such a one would have ripped up the most nasty
vice that ever hell belched forth, and presented it to a modest assembly.
Yet we rather wish in such discoveries, where reputation lies bleeding,
a slackness of truth than fulness of slander.

Thomas Middleton, *The Roaring Girl*, 1601,
Introduction

23   A playwright on the players

Hamlet's famous comments on contemporary acting is of perennial interest to students of the theatre of his own age and ours.

Speak the speech, I pray you, as I pronounc'd it to you, trippingly on the tongue; but if you mouth it, as many of our players do, I had as lief the town-crier spoke my lines. Nor do not saw the air too much with your hand, thus, but use all gently; for in the very torrent, tempest, and, as I may say, whirlwind of your passion, you must acquire and beget a temperance that may give it smoothness. O, it offends me to the soul to hear a robustious periwig-pated fellow tear a passion to tatters, to very rags to split the ears of the groundlings, who, for the most part, are capable of nothing but inexplicable dumb shows and noise. I would have such a fellow whipp'd for o'erdoing Termagant; it out-herods Herod. Pray you avoid it.

1 Player: I warrant your honour.

Hamlet: Be not too tame neither, but let your own discretion be your tutor. Suit the action to the word, the word to the action; with this special observance, that you o'erstep not the modesty of nature; for anything so o'erdone is from the purpose of playing, whose end, both at the first and now, was and is to hold, as 'twere, the mirror up to nature; to show virtue her own feature, scorn her own image, and the very age and body of the time his form and pressure. Now, this overdone or come tardy off, though it makes the unskilful laugh, cannot but make the judicious grieve; the censure of the which one must, in your allowance, o'ereweigh a whole theatre of others. Oh, there be players that I have seen play—and heard others praise, and that highly—not to speak it profanely, that, neither having th' accent of Christians, nor the gait of Christian, pagan, nor man, have so strutted and bellowed that I have thought some of Nature's journeymen had made men, and not made them well, they imitated humanity so abominably.

1 Player: I hope we have reform'd that indifferently with us, sir.

Hamlet: O, reform it altogether. And let those that play your clowns speak no more than is set down for them; for there be of them that will themselves laugh, to set on some quantity of barren spectators to laugh too, though in the meantime some necessary question of the play be then to be considered. That's

villainous, and shows a most pitiful ambition in the fool that uses
it. Go, make you ready.   [Exeunt Players.]

                          Hamlet, III, 2

24   The other side of the theatre

This extract from *The School of Abuse*, a famous attack on the theatre, reflects
the growing alarm aroused by both plays and their audiences. The gathering
Puritan hostility reached its climax with the official closing of theatres by
Parliament in 1642. Gosson in his younger days had been a playwright but
ended his life as a clergyman in the Church of England.

In our assemblies at plays in London, you shall see such heaving,
and shoving, such itching and shouldering to sit by women: such
care for their garments, that they be not trod on: such eyes to their
laps, that no chips light in them: such pillows to their backs, that they
take no hurt: such masking in their ears, I know not what: such giving
them pippins to pass the time: such playing at foot-saunt without cards:
such tickling, such toying, such smiling, such winking, and such
manning them home, when the sports are ended, that it is a right
comedy to mark their behaviour, to watch their conceits, as the cat
for the mouse, and as good as a course at the game itself, to dog them
a little, or follow aloof by the print of their feet, and so discover
by slot where the deer taketh soil. If this were as well noted as ill seen,
or as openly punished as secretly practised, I have no doubt but the
cause would be seared to dry up the effect, and these pretty rabbits
very cunningly ferreted from their burrows. For they that lack
customers all the week, either because their haunt is unknown or the
constables and officers of their parish watch them so narrowly that
they dare not quetch, to celebrate the sabbath flock to theatres, and
there keep a general market of bawdry. Not that any filthiness in
deed is committed within the compass of that ground, as was done in
Rome, but that every wanton and his paramour, every man and his
mistress, every John and his Joan, every knave and his quean, are
there first acquainted and cheapen the merchandise in that place, which
they pay for elsewhere as they can agree.

Stephen Gosson, *The School of Abuse*, 1579,
cited in *Life in Shakespeare's England*, ed.
J. Dover Wilson (Pelican ed., 1944), p. 169

25 The joy of poetry

We print below two famous passages which concern Sir Philip Sidney (nephew of the Earl of Leicester), the paradigm of an Elizabethan courtier. The first is his memorable evocation of the poet; the second, written by his friend, Fulke Greville, describes Sidney's behaviour on the battlefield where he was fatally wounded.

(i) Now therein of all sciences (I speak still of human, and according to the human conceits) is our poet the monarch. For he doth not only show the way, but giveth so sweet a prospect into the way, as will entice any man to enter into it. Nay, he doth, as if your journey should lie through a fair vineyard, at the first give you a cluster of grapes, that full of that taste, you may long to pass further. He beginneth not with obscure definitions, which must blur the margent with interpretations, and load the memory with doubtfulness; but he cometh to you with words set in delightful proportion, either accompanied with, or prepared for, the well enchanting skill of music; and with a tale forsooth he cometh unto you, with a tale which holdeth children from play, and old men from the chimney corner.

Philip Sidney, *An Apology for Poetry*, ed. G. Shepherd (1965), p. 113

(ii) Howsoever, by this stand, an unfortunate hand out of those forespoken trenches, brake the bone of Sir Philip's thigh with a musketshot. The horse he rode upon, was rather furiously choleric than bravely proud, and so forced him to forsake the field, but not his back, as the noblest and fittest bier to carry a martial commander to his grave. In which sad progress, passing along by the rest of the army, where his uncle the general was, and being thirsty with excess of bleeding, he called for drink, which was presently brought him; but as he was putting the bottle to his mouth, he saw a poor soldier carried along, who had eaten his last at the same feast, ghastly casting up his eyes at the bottle. Which Sir Philip perceiving, took it from his head, before he drank, and delivered it to the poor man, with these words, 'Thy necessity is yet greater than mine.' And when he had pledged this poor soldier, he was presently carried to Arnhem.

Fulke Greville, Lord Brooke, *The Life of the renowned Sir Philip Sidney*, in *Works*, ed. A. B. Grosart (1870), iv, 130–31

26   Pop poetry: late Elizabethan

This ballad, paying tribute to Sir Francis Drake's circum-navigation of the world (1577–80), was written, in fact, some years after the event since it refers to the loss at sea of Sir Humphrey Gilbert in 1584.

Sir Francis, Sir Francis, Sir Francis is come;
Sir Robert and eke Sir William his son,
And eke the good Earl Huntington
March'd gallantly on the Road.

Then came the Lord Chamberlain with his white staff,
And all the people began to laugh;
And then the Queen began to speak,
'You're welcome home, Sir Francis Drake.'

You gallants all o' the British blood,
Why don't you sail o' th' ocean flood?
I protest you're not all worth a filbert,
If once compared to Sir Humphrey Gilbert.

For he went out on a rainy day,
And to the new found land found out his way,
With many a gallant both fresh and green,
And he ne'er came home again. God bless the Queen!

F. J. Furnivall, Ballads from Manuscripts
(Hertford, 1873), ii, 100–101

27   The new astronomy comes to England

The second half of the sixteenth century and the first half of the seventeenth saw the vigorous debate between the exponents of the Copernican doctrine that the earth went round the sun, and those who upheld the older Ptolemaic interpretation that the earth was the centre of the universe. Here the mathematician, Thomas Digges, revising the work of his father, Leonard Digges, begins his lively defence of the Copernican standpoint.

Having of late, gentle Reader, corrected and reformed sundry faults that by negligence in printing have crept into my father's General Prognostication, among other things I found a description or model of the world and situation of spheres celestial and elementary according to the doctrine of Ptolemy, whereunto all universities (led thereto chiefly by the authority of Aristotle) since then have consented. But in this our age one rare wit (seeing the continual errors that from time to time more and more have been discovered, besides the infinite absurdities in their theorickes, which they have been forced to admit that would not confess any mobility in the ball of the earth) hath by long study, painful practise, and rare invention delivered a new theorick or model of the world, shewing that the earth resteth not in the centre of the whole world, but only in the centre of this our mortal world or globe of elements, which environed and enclosed in the moon's orb, and together with the whole globe of mortality is carried yearly round about the sun, which like a king in the midst of all reigneth and giveth the laws of motion to the rest, spherically dispersing his glorious beams of light through all this sacred celestial temple. And the earth itself to be one of the planets, having his peculiar and straying courses turning every twenty-four hours round upon his own centre, whereby the sun and great globe of fixed stars seem to sway about and turn, albeit indeed they remain fixed.

So many ways is the sense of mortal men abused, but reason and deep discourse of wit having opened these things to Copernicus, and the same being with demonstrations mathematical most apparently by him to the world delivered, I thought it convenient together with the old theorick also to publish this, to the end such noble English minds (as delight to reach above the baser sort of men) might not be altogether defrauded of so noble a part of philosophy. And to the end it might manifestly appear that Copernicus meant not, as some have fondly excused him, to deliver these grounds of the earth's mobility only as mathematical principles, feigned and not as philosophical truly averred.

> Thomas Digges, *Prognostication everlasting*, in F. R. Johnson and S. V. Larkey, 'Thomas Digges, the Copernican system and the idea of the infinity of the universe in 1576', *Hunt. Lib. Bull.*, now *Quarterly* (1934), pp. 69–117: modernised in H. Haydn, *The Portable Elizabethan Reader* (N.Y., 1955), pp. 106–25

28 Another view of the new astronomy

More than half a century after the work of Copernicus the old doctrines about the sun encircling the earth are still firmly held. The writer of this passage has misdated the book. The *De Revolutionibus Orbium Caelestium* was published in 1543 not 1536.

Some also deny that the earth is in the midst of the world, and some affirm that it is moveable, as also Copernicus—by way of supposition, and not for that he thought so indeed—who affirmed that the earth turneth about and that the sun standeth still in the midst of the heavens; by help of which false supposition he hath made truer demonstrations of the motions and revolutions of the celestial spheres than ever were made before, as plainly appeareth by his book *De Revolutionibus*, dedicated to the Pope in the year of our Lord 1536. But Ptolemy, Aristotle and all other old writers affirm the earth to be in the midst, and to remain unmoveable and to be in the very centre of the world, proving the same with many most strong reasons not needful here to be rehearsed, because I think few or none do doubt thereof, and specially the Holy Scripture affirming the foundations of the Earth to be laid so sure that it never should move at any time.

> Thomas Blundevile, *M. Blundevile his exercises* (1594), fol. 181 recto, cited in A. Nicoll, *The Elizabethans* (Cambridge, 1957), p. 14

29　The discovery of a new herb

This late sixteenth-century account of the arrival of tobacco from the New World and its planting in Europe provides a picture of its early reception and the medicinal qualities attributed to it. It was not long, however, before contemporaries were drawing attention to it as a cause of personal and public pollution. Thomas Hariot, the eminent mathematician and explorer, is thought to have been the first man to have died of cancer arising from nicotine.

It is usually larger than our comfrey, though found flourishing in the same well-watered spots of rich earth, exposed to the sun. It has very wide leaves, of oblong shape, hairy quality, wider, rounder, larger than those of comfrey. . . . The stalk grows three cubits high in France, Belgium and England, and very often four or five cubits when it is sown early enough in warmer parts of Aquitaine and Languedoc. It bears flower calyxes in August of a pale, somewhat reddish green. . . . For you will observe shipmasters [sailors] and all others who come back from out there [i.e. America] using little funnels, made of palm leaves or straw, in the extreme end of which they stuff [crumbled dried leaves] of this plant. This they light, and opening their mouths as much as they can, they suck in the smoke with their breath. By this they say their hunger and thirst are allayed, their strength restored, and their spirits refreshed. . . . Our age has discovered nothing from the New World which will be numbered among the remedies more valuable and efficacious than this plant for sores, wounds, affections of the throat and chest, and the fever of the plague.

Tobacco, Its History . . . , ed. J. E. Brooks, (New York, 1937–52), i, 239–40, cited in F. D. and J. F. M. Hoeniger, *The Development of Natural History in Tudor England*, Folger Shakespeare Library (Virginia, 1969), p. 54

30 Helpful hints for sickly children

Lord Herbert of Cherbury, courtier and diplomat under James I and Charles I, luckless and disappointed in his hopes of advancement, wrote a fascinating, and boastful, *Autobiography* in which he drew heavily on both his memory and his imagination. Here he gives some medical advice which, in passing, provides an alarming picture of both the diseases of childhood and their treatment. The nurse referred to is a wet-nurse: it was customary for upper-class children to be fed in this way in infancy.

And first, I find, that in the infancy those diseases are to be remedied which may be hereditary unto them on either side; so that, if they be subject to the stone or gravel, I do conceive it will be good for the nurse sometimes to drink posset drinks, in which are boiled such things as are good to expel gravel and stone; the child also himself when he comes to some age may use the same posset drinks of herbs, as milium solis, saxifragia, etc., good for the stone many are reckoned by the physicians, of which also myself could bring a large catalogue, but rather leave it to those who are expert in that art. The same course is to be taken for the gout; for which purpose I do much commend the bathing of children's legs and feet in the water wherein smiths quench their iron, as also water wherein alum hath been infused, or boiled, as also the decoction of juniper berries, bay berries, chamæ-drys, chemæpitys, which baths also are good for those that are heredi-tarily subject to the palsy, for these things do much strengthen the sinews; as also olium castorii, and sucini, which are not to be used without advice. They that are also subject to the spleen from their ancestors, ought to use those herbs that are splenetics: and those that are troubled with the falling sickness, with cephaniques, of which certainly I should have had need but for the purging of my ears above mentioned. Briefly, what disease soever it be that is derived from ancestors of either side, it will be necessary first to give such medicines to the nurse as may make her milk effectual for those purposes; as also afterwards to give unto the child itself such specific remedies as his age and constitution will bear. I could say much more upon this point, as having delighted ever in the knowledge of herbs, plants, and gums, and in few words the history of nature, insomuch, that coming to apothecaries' shops, it was my ordinary manner when I looked upon the bills filed up, containing the physicians' prescriptions, to tell every man's disease; howbeit, I shall not presume in these particulars to prescribe to my posterity, though I believe I know the best receipts for almost all diseases, but shall leave them to the expert physician; only I will recommend again to my posterity the curing of hereditary diseases in the very infancy, since, otherwise, without much difficulty, they will never be cured.

> The Autobiography of Edward, Lord Herbert of
> Cherbury, ed. S. Lee (2nd. ed., n.d.), pp.
> 23–4

31   The sad state of the medical profession

In this passage from the *Advancement of Learning*, published by Francis Bacon, two years after the death of Queen Elizabeth, he coments on the backwardness of medical science. The end of this extract is followed by a detailed criticism of its methods of treatment and research.

Nay, we see the weakness and credulity of men is such, as they will often prefer a mountebank or witch before a learned physician. . . . And what followeth? Even this, that physicians say to themselves, as Solomon expresseth it upon an higher occasion: 'If it befal me as befalleth to the fools, why should I labour to be more wise?' And therefore I cannot much blame physicians that they use commonly to intend some other art or practice, which they fancy, more than their profession. For you shall have them antiquaries, poets, humanists, statesmen, merchants, divines, and in every of these better seen than in their profession; and no doubt upon this ground, that they find that mediocrity and excellency in their art maketh no difference in profit or reputation towards their fortune. . . .

Medicine is a science which hath been (as we have said) more professed than laboured, and yet more laboured than advanced; the labour having been, in my judgement, rather in circle than in progression. For I find much iteration, but small addition.

> J. Spedding, *et. al.* (eds.), *The Works of Francis
> Bacon* (1857), iii, 371–3

32 The impact of modern science

This extract from a poem by John Donne, written in 1611, displays the profound effects upon the traditional outlook made by recent discoveries in astronomy. Donne sees these developments as part of a crumbling of the whole social order; but the poem reflects also his own transition from an Elizabethan courtly poet of moving tenderness and sensuality to his later phase when, a priest in Holy Orders and finally Dean of St. Paul's, he expressed his deep searching into the nature of man and the universe.

> Then, as mankind, so is the world's whole frame
> Quite out of joint, almost created lame.
> For before God hath made up all the rest,
> Corruption entered and depraved the best. . . .
> And new philosophy calls all in doubt,
> The element of fire is quite put out;
> The sun is lost, and th'earth, and no man's wit
> Can well direct him where to look for it.
> And freely men confess that this world's spent,
> When in the planets, and the firmament
> They seek so many new; then see that this
> Is crumbled out again to his Atomies.
> 'Tis all in pieces, all coherence gone;
> All just supply, and all relation.
> Prince, subject, father, son are things forgot,
> For every man alone thinks he hath got
> To be a phoenix, and that then can be
> None of that kind, of which he is, but he.
> This is the world's condition now. . . .'

John Donne, *An Anatomy of the World*, The First Anniversary, in *John Donne, Complete Poetry and Selected Prose*, ed. J. Hayward (1930), pp. 202–3

IV

RELIGION

1 The royal supremacy

The act of Supremacy, as finally passed by Elizabeth's first parliament in 1559, abolished all foreign ecclesiastical jurisdiction in England, annexed such jurisdiction to the Crown 'by authority' of parliament, gave parliamentary permission for the delegation of that royal supremacy over the Church, and provided that all ecclesiastics and royal officials should take an oath which recognised the Queen as 'supreme governor' of the realm in 'all spiritual or ecclesiastical' as well as in all temporal matters. The royal supremacy thus established differed in two important ways from that enjoyed by Henry VIII and Edward VI. The Henrician supremacy over the Church had been merely *recognised* not *conferred* by parliament; and Henry and Edward had both borne the title of 'supreme head' of the Church with all its quasi-episcopal overtones. Elizabeth, as supreme governor, was very clearly a lay personage ruling the Church from outside, not a kind of unconsecrated bishop controlling it from within, as her father had been. Moreover, as her supremacy had been authorised by parliament, the House of Commons throughout her reign was able to assume a right to interfere in the government and administration of the Church—a claim which the Queen never recognised, but which was much more plausible than it would have been in her father's reign.

The act was ameliorated in several respects in practice. For example, the corporal oath, i.e. the physical touching of the testament with the hand, was not always administered to the Queen's officials and some Catholics were therefore able to continue in her service.

VII. And to the intent that all usurped and foreign power and authority, spiritual and temporal, may for ever be clearly extinguished and never to be used nor obeyed within this realm or any other your Majesty's dominions or countries: May it please your Highness that it may be further enacted by the authority aforesaid [i.e. Parliament] that no foreign prince, person, prelate, state or potentate, spiritual or temporal, shall at any time after the last day of this session of Parliament use, enjoy or exercise any manner of power, jurisdiction, superiority, authority, pre-eminence or privilege spiritual or ecclesiastical, within

this realm or within any other your Majesty's dominions or countries
that now be or hereafter shall be, but from thenceforth the same
shall be clearly abolished out of this realm and all other your Highness'
dominions for ever; any statute, ordinance, custom, constitutions or
any other matter or cause whatsoever to the contrary in any wise
notwithstanding.

VIII. And that also it may likewise please your Highness that it
may be established and enacted by the authority aforesaid that such
jurisdictions, privileges, superiorities and pre-eminences spiritual
and ecclesiastical, as by any spiritual or ecclesiastical power or authority
hath heretofore been or may lawfully be exercised or used for the
visitation of the ecclesiastical state and persons, and for reformation,
order and correction of the same and of all manner of errors, heresies,
schisms, abuses, offences, contempts and enormities, shall for ever
by authority of this present Parliament be united and annexed to the
imperial crown of this realm. And that your Highness, your heirs and
successors, kings or queens of this realm, shall have full power and
authority, by virtue of this act, by letters patents under the great seal
of England to assign, name and authorise, when and as often as your
Highness, your heirs or successors, shall think meet and convenient,
and for such and so long time as shall please your Highness, your heirs
or successors, such person or persons being natural born subjects to
your Highness, your heirs or successors, as your Majesty, your heirs
or successors, shall think meet, to exercise, use, occupy and execute
under your Highness, your heirs and successors, all manner of jurisdictions, privileges and preeminences in any wise touching or concerning
any spiritual or ecclesiastical jurisdiction within these your realms . . .
and to visit, reform, redress, order, correct and amend all such errors,
heresies, schisms, abuses, offences, contempts and enormities whatsoever which by any manner spiritual or ecclesiastical power, authority
or jurisdiction can or may lawfully be reformed, ordered, redressed,
corrected, restrained, or amended, to the pleasure of Almighty God,
the increase of virtue, and the conservation of the peace and unity
of this realm. And that such person or persons so to be named, assigned,
authorised and appointed by your Highness, your heirs or successors,
after the said letter patents to him or them made and delivered as is
aforesaid, shall have full power and authority, by virtue of this act
and of the said letters patents, under your Highness, your heirs or
successors, to exercise, use and execute all the premises according to the
tenor and effect of the said letters patents; any matter or cause to the
contrary in any wise notwithstanding.

IX. And for the better observation and maintenance of this act, may it please your Highness that it may be further enacted by the authority aforesaid that all and every archbishop, bishop, and all and every other ecclesiastical person and other ecclesiastical officer and minister, of what estate, dignity, preeminence or degree soever he or they be or shall be, and all and every temporal judge, justicer, mayor and other lay or temporal officer and minister, and every other person having your Highness' fee or wages within this realm or any your Highness' dominions, shall make, take and receive a corporal oath upon the evangelist, before such person or persons as shall please your Highness, your heirs or successors, under the great seal of England to assign and name to accept and take the same, according to the tenor and effect hereafter following, that is to say:

I, *A.B.*, do utterly testify and declare in my conscience that the Queen's Highness is the only supreme governor of this realm and of all other her Highness' dominions and countries, as well in all spiritual or ecclesiastical things or causes as temporal, and that no foreign prince, person, prelate, state or potentate hath or ought to have any jurisdiction, power, superiority, preeminence or authority ecclesiastical or spiritual within this realm, and therefore I do utterly renounce and forsake all foreign jurisdictions, powers, superiorities and authorities, and do promise that from henceforth I shall bear faith and true allegiance to the Queen's Highness, her heirs and lawful successors, and to my power shall assist and defend all jurisdictions, preeminences, privileges and authorities granted or belonging to the Queen's Highness, her heirs and successors, or united or annexed to the imperial crown of this realm: so help me God and by the contents of this Book.

1 Eliz. c. 1, *Statutes of the Realm*, iv, 352

2   Doctrinal uniformity

The act of Uniformity of 1559 re-introduced Edward VI's 1552 Prayer Book as the basis of English worship, though it made three changes which took account of the attitude of the Queen, who would have preferred the more conservative Book of 1549. Two of the alterations, the additions to the lessons to be said on Sundays and the changes in the Litany, were of minor importance, but the third, the addition of the words of communion from the 1549 Prayer Book to those of the 1552 Prayer Book, was of very great significance as it allowed the recipient of the sacrament a belief in the real presence short of transubstantiation. Clause thirteen of the act, which provided that the ministers of the Church should wear the vestments which had been in use by authority of parliament in the second year of Edward VI, was ambiguous, as it was uncertain whether or not it was intended to refer to the first Edwardian Prayer Book of 1549, which belonged to Edward's third year. Whatever the exact intention of this clause it certainly imposed, at least in theory and until further royal orders, the use of medieval mass vestments. It led to the vestiarian controversy which divided the Church in the 1560s.

Where at the death of our late sovereign lord King Edward the Sixth there remained one uniform order of common service and prayer and of the administration of sacraments, rites and ceremonies in the Church of England, which was set forth in one book entitled The Book of Common Prayer and Administration of Sacraments and other Rites and Ceremonies in the Church of England, authorised by act of Parliament holden in the fifth and sixth years of our said late sovereign lord King Edward the Sixth, entitled an Act for the Uniformity of Common Prayer and Administration of the Sacraments; the which was repealed and taken away by act of Parliament in the first year of the reign of our late sovereign lady Queen Mary, to the great decay of the due honour of God and discomfort to the professors of the truth of Christ's religion: Be it therefore enacted by the authority of this present Parliament that the said statute of repeal and everything therein contained only concerning the said book and the service, administration of sacraments, rites and ceremonies contained or appointed in or by the said book, shall be void and of none effect from and after the feast of the Nativity of St. John Baptist next coming; and that the said book with the order of service and of the administration of sacraments, rites and ceremonies, with the alteration and additions therein added and appointed by this statute, shall stand and be from and after the said feast . . . in full force and effect according to the tenor and effect of this statute; anything in the aforesaid statute of repeal to the contrary notwithstanding.

II. And further be it enacted by the Queen's Highness, with the assent of the Lords and Commons in this present Parliament assembled and by authority of the same, that all and singular ministers in any cathedral or parish church or other place within this realm of England, Wales and the marches of the same, or other the Queen's dominions, shall, from and after the feast of the Nativity of St. John Baptist next coming, be bounden to say and use the matins, evensong, celebration of the Lord's supper and administration of each of the sacraments, and all their common and open prayer, in such order and form as is mentioned in the said book so authorised by Parliament in the said fifth and sixth year of the reign of King Edward the Sixth, with one alteration or addition of certain lessons to be used on every Sunday in the year, and the form of the Litany altered and corrected, and two sentences only added in the delivery of the sacrament to the communicants, and none other or otherwise. . . .

XIII. Provided always and be it enacted that such ornaments of the Church, and of the ministers thereof shall be retained and be in use as was in the Church of England by authority of Parliament in the second year of the reign of King Edward the Sixth until other order shall be therein taken by the authority of the Queen's Majesty, with the advice of her commissioners appointed and authorised under the great seal of England for causes ecclesiastical, or of the metropolitan of this realm. . . .

1 Eliz. c. 2, *Statutes of the Realm*, iv, 355–8

3   The administration of the Church

The settlement of 1559, while imposing a royal supremacy and Protestant form of worship upon the Church, left intact its traditional administrative structure, inherited from the Middle Ages. It was this form of organisation which the more extreme Puritans, under the leadership of Thomas Cartwright, rejected as unscriptural from the 1570s onwards.

The Church of England is divided into two provinces: Canterbury and York.
The province of Canterbury hath
The archbishop of the same, who is primate of all England and metropolitan,
The bishop of London,
The bishop of

Winchester	Exeter
Ely	Rochester
Chichester	Peterborough
Hereford	St. Davids
Salisbury	St. Asaph
Worcester	Llandaff
Lincoln	Bangor
Coventry and Lichfield	Oxford
Bath and Wells	Gloucester, and
Norwich	Bristol

The province of York hath
The archbishop of the same, who is also primate of England and metropolitan,
The bishop of Durham, Carlisle and Chester
Amongst us here in England no man is called or preferred to be a bishop except he have first been instituted a priest or minister and be well able to instruct the people in the Holy Scriptures.

Every one of the archbishops and bishops have their several cathedral churches, wherein the deans bear chief rule, being men specially chosen both for their learning and godliness, as near as may be.

These cathedral churches have also other dignities and canonries, whereunto be assigned no idle or unprofitable persons but such as either be preachers or professors of the sciences of good learning. . . .

Also the said archbishops and bishops have under them their archdeacons, some two, some four, some six, according to the largeness of the diocese; the which archdeacons keep yearly two visitations, therein they make diligent inquisition and search both of the doctrine and behaviour as well of the ministers as of the people. They punish the offenders; and, if any errors in religion and heresies fortune to spring, they bring those and other weighty matters before the bishops themselves.

> John Jewel, *An Apology of the Church of England*, ed. J. E. Booty, Folger Shakespeare Library (Ithaca, 1963), pp. 139–40

4 Henrician and Elizabethan supremacies contrasted

This act brings out clearly the difference between the theoretical nature of the Henrician and Edwardian supremacy over the Church on the one hand and the Elizabethan on the other, the former an existing right which was merely 'recognized and knowledged' by parliament, the latter a power established 'by the authority of . . . parliament'.

Forasmuch as divers questions by overmuch boldness of speech and talk amongst many of the common sort of people being unlearned have lately grown upon the making and consecrating of archbishops and bishops within this realm, whether the same were and be duly and orderly done according to the law or not, which is much tending to the slander of all the state of the clergy, being one of the greatest states of this realm. Therefore, for the avoiding of such slanderous speech and to the intent that every man that is willing to know the truth may plainly understand that the same evil speech and talk is not grounded upon any just matter or cause, it is thought convenient hereby partly to touch such authorities as doth allow and approve the making and consecrating of the same archbishops and bishops to be duly and orderly done according to the laws of this realm and thereupon further to provide for the more surety thereof as hereafter shall be expressed.

First, it is very well known to all degrees of this realm that the late king of most famous memory, King Henry the Eighth, as well by all the clergy then of this realm in their several convocations, as also by all the Lords Spiritual and Temporal and Commons assembled in divers of his parliaments, was justly and rightfully recognized and knowledged to have the supreme power, jurisdiction, order, rule and authority over all the states ecclesiastical of the same, and the same power, jurisdiction and authority did use accordingly; and that also the said late king, in the 25th year of his reign, did by authority of parliament amongst other things set forth a certain order of the manner and form how archbishops and bishops within this realm and other his dominions should be elected and made, as by the same more plainly appeareth. And that also the late king of worthy memory, King Edward the Sixth, did lawfully succeed the said late King Henry his father in the Imperial Crown of this realm and did justly possess and enjoy all the same power, jurisdiction and authority before mentioned as a thing to him descended with the same imperial crown, and so used the same during his life. And that also the said late King Edward the Sixth in his time by authority of parliament caused a godly and virtuous book entitled The Book of Common Prayer . . . to be made and set forth, not only for one uniform order of service . . . to be used within all this realm and other his dominions, but also did add and put to the same book a very good and godly order of the manner and form how archbishops, bishops, priests, deacons and ministers should from time to time be consecrated, made and ordered within this realm and other his dominions, as by the same more plainly may and will appear. And although in the time of the late Queen Mary, as well the said act and statute made in the 25th year of the reign of the said late King Henry the Eighth, as also the several acts and statutes made in the second, third, fourth, fifth, and sixth years of the reign of the said late King Edward, for the authorising and allowing of the said Book of Common Prayer and other the premises amongst divers other acts and statutes touching the said supreme authority, were repealed, yet, nevertheless, at the parliament holden at Westminster in the first year of the reign of our sovereign lady the Queen's Majesty that now is, by one other act and statute there made, all such jurisdictions, privileges, superiorities and pre-eminences spiritual and ecclesiastical as by any spiritual or ecclesiastical power or authority hath heretofore been or may be lawfully used over the ecclesiastical estate of this realm, and the order, reformation and correction of the same is fully and absolutely by the authority of the same parliament, united and annexed to the imperial crown of this realm. And by the same act and statute there is also given to the Queen's Highness, her heirs and successors, kings or queens of this realm, full power and authority, by letters patents under the Great Seal of England, from time to time to assign, name and authorise such person or persons as she or they shall think meet and convenient to exercise, use, occupy and execute under her Highness all manner of jurisdictions, privileges, pre-eminences and authorities in any wise touching or concerning any spiritual or ecclesiastical power or jurisdiction within this realm or any other her Highness's dominions or countries. . . .

8 Eliz. c. 1, *Statutes of the Realm*, iv, 484–5

5 The High Commission of 1559

The exercise of the royal supremacy was delegated by the Queen during her reign, in accordance with the act of Supremacy, to a series of High Commissions, of which the first was established in 1559. It soon—probably in the 1560s—became a formal court, but its jurisdiction was much resented by Puritans who objected to its procedure and complained that it exceeded its proper powers. The common law judges, however, confirmed the court's claims and status by their decision in Cawdrey's case in 1591.

Elizabeth by the grace of God [etc.]. To the reverend father in God Matthew Parker, nominated bishop of Canterbury and Edmund Grindal, nominated bishop of London, and to our right trusted and right well-beloved councillors [17 names given], greeting.

Where at our parliament holden at Westminster the 25th day of January and there continued and kept until the eighth of May then next following, amongst other things there was two acts and statutes made and established, the one entitled, 'An act for the uniformity of common prayer [etc.]', and the other entitled, 'An act restoring to the Crown the ancient jurisdiction [etc.]', as by the same several acts more at large doth appear: and where divers seditious and slanderous persons do not cease daily to invent and set forth false rumours, tales, and seditious slanders, not only against us and the said good laws and statutes, but also have set forth divers seditious books within this our realm of England, meaning thereby to move and procure strife, division and dissension amongst our loving and obedient subjects much to the disquieting of us and our people.

Wherefore, we, earnestly minding to have the same acts before mentioned to be duly put in execution, and such persons as shall hereafter offend in anything contrary to the tenor and effect of the said several statutes to be condignly punished, and having especial trust and confidence in your wisdoms and discretions, have authorised, assigned and appointed you to be our commissioners, and by these presents do give our full power and authority to you, or six of you, whereof you, the said Matthew Parker, Edmund Grindal, Thomas Smith, Walter Haddon, Thomas Sackford, Richard Goodrich and Gilbert Gerrard to be one, from time to time hereafter during our pleasure, to enquire as well by the oaths of twelve good and lawful men, as also by witnesses and all other ways and means ye can devise for all offences, misdoers [sic] and misdemeanours done and committed and hereafter to be committed or done contrary to the tenor and effect of the said several acts and statutes and either of them and also of all and singular heretical opinions, seditious books, contempts, conspiracies, false rumours, tales, seditions, misbehaviours, slanderous words or shewings, published, invented, or set forth, or hereafter to be published invented or set forth by any person or persons against us or contrary or against any the laws or statutes of this our realm, or against the quiet governance and rule of our people and subjects in any county, city, borough or other place or places within this our realm of England, and of all and every the coadjutors, counsellors, comforters, procurers and abettors of every such offender.

Select Statutes, ed. G. W. Prothero (1898), pp. 227–8

6 A protest from Burghley

The aspect of High Commission procedure which aroused most general resentment was undoubtedly the *ex officio* oath, which compelled those under examination to promise to answer truthfully any charges which might be preferred against them before they knew what those charges were. This in effect required men to incriminate themselves. It was a civil law procedure foreign to the tradition of the English common law and it is significant that it aroused distaste among men who were loyal Anglicans: witness Burghley's letter to Whitgift in the summer of 1584.

'. . . But now, my good lord, I am come to the sight of an instrument of twenty-four articles of great length and curiosity, found in a Romish style, to examine all manner of ministers in this time without distinction of persons. Which articles are entitled, *apud Lambeth*, *May 1584, to be executed ex officio mero, etc.* . . . I sent for the register, who brought me the articles, which I have read and find so curiously penned, so full of branches and circumstances as I think the inquisitors of Spain use not so many questions to comprehend and trap their preys.

I know your canonists can defend these with all their particles, but surely, under your grace's correction, this judicial and canonical sifting of poor ministers is not to edify or reform. And in charity, I think they ought not to answer to all these nice points, except they were very notorious offenders in papistry or heresy. Now, my good lord, bear with my scribbling. I write with a testimony of a good conscience. I desire the peace of the church. I desire concord and unity in the exercise of our religion. I favour no sensual and wilful recusants. But I conclude that, according to my simple judgment, this kind of proceeding is too much savouring of the Romish inquisition and is rather a device to seek for offenders than to reform any. . . .'

Lord Burghley to Archbishop Whitgift, 1 July 1584, in J. Strype, *The Life and Acts of John Whitgift* (1822), iii, 105–6

7 The High Commission confirmed

Puritan hostility to the Court of High Commission culminated in Robert Cawdrey's action in Queen's Bench in 1591. Cawdrey, a clergyman, had been deprived for nonconformity by the High Commission and the essence of his plea was that the Commission had exceeded the powers it possessed under the act of Supremacy. The decision went against him, as the Queen's Bench judges affirmed that the act of Supremacy did not circumscribe the powers of the Crown in ecclesiastical jurisdiction and that the authority of the Court of High Commission therefore depended on the terms of the royal letters patent which had created it. These letters patent had given the Court very wide authority and the decision of 1591 effectively established the High Commission as both a lawful and a powerful court. It is of interest that Sir Edward Coke, one of the greatest defenders of English common law, fully acknowledged here the authority of the Court of High Commission.

It was resolved by all the judges that the king or queen of England for the time being may make such an ecclesiastical commission as is before mentioned by the ancient prerogative and law of England. And therefore by the ancient laws of this realm this kingdom of England is an absolute empire and monarchy consisting of one head, which is the king, and of a body politic compact and compounded of many and almost infinite several and yet well agreeing members; all which the law divideth into two general parts, that is to say, the clergy and the laity, both of them, next and immediately under God, subject and obedient to the head. Also the kingly head of this politic body is instituted and furnished with plenary and entire power, prerogative and jurisdiction to render justice and right to every part and member of this body, of what estate, degree, or calling soever, in all causes ecclesiastical or temporal, otherwise he should not be a head of the whole body. And as in temporal causes the king by the mouth of the judges in his courts of justice doth judge and determine the same by the temporal laws of England, so in causes ecclesiastical and spiritual, as namely blasphemy, apostasy from Christianity, heresies, schisms, ordering admissions, institutions of clerks, celebration of divine service, rights of matrimony, divorces, general bastardy, subtraction and right of tithes, oblations, obventions, dilapidations, reparation of churches, probates of testaments, administrations and accounts upon the same, simony, incests, fornications, adulteries, solicitation of chastity, pensions, procurations, appeals in ecclesiastical causes, commutation of penance, and others (the cognizance whereof belongs not to the common laws of England) the same are to be determined and decided by ecclesiastical judges, according to the king's ecclesiastical laws of this realm. . . .

The Fifth Part of the Reports of Sir Edward Coke (1738 ed.), pp. viii–ix

8   Royal reflections on the Church

Here is another example of the Queen's determination to resist what she regarded as unwarranted parliamentary interference in ecclesiastical affairs. Her own attitude towards the Church, as this speech of 1585 to the assembled Lords and Commons shows, was essentially a pragmatic one. She realised that abuses were bound to grow in the Church—'what vocation without', as she put it— but thought that these should be discreetly amended by the clergy under her own supervision. She also took this opportunity to make it very clear that she was unalterably opposed to both Catholicism and Puritanism.

... One matter toucheth me so near as I may not overskip; religion, the ground on which all other matters ought to take root, and being corrupted, may mar all the tree; and that there be some fault-finders with the order of the clergy, which so may make a slander to myself and the church, whose over-ruler God hath made me, whose negligence cannot be excused if any schisms or errors heretical were suffered. Thus much I must say, that some faults and negligences may grow and be, as in all other great charges it happeneth, and what vocation without? All which if you, my lords of the clergy, do not amend, I mean to depose you. Look ye therefore well to your charges. This may be amended without heedless or open exclamations. I am supposed to have many studies, but most philosophical. I must yield this to be true, that I suppose few (that be no professors) have read more. And I need not tell you, that I am so simple that I understand not, nor so forgetful that I remember not; and yet amidst my many volumes I hope God's book hath not been my seldomest lectures, in which we find that which by reason (for my part) we ought to believe: that seeing so great wickedness and griefs in the world in which we live but as wayfaring pilgrims, we must suppose that God would never have made us but for a better place and of more comfort than we find here. . . . I see many over-bold with God Almighty, making too many subtle scannings of His blessed will, as lawyers do with human testaments. The presumption is so great as I may not suffer it. Yet mind I not hereby to animate Romanists (which what adversaries they be to mine estate is sufficiently known) nor tolerate new-fangleness. I mean to guide them both by God's holy true rule. In both parts be perils, and of the latter I must pronounce them dangerous to a kingly rule, to have every man according to his own censure to make a doom of the validity and privity of his prince's government with a common veil and cover of God's word, whose followers must not be judged but by private men's exposition. God defend you from such a ruler that so evil will guide you. . . .

> The Queen to the assembled Lords and Commons in parliament, 29 March 1585, in S. D'Ewes, *Journals* (1682), pp. 328–9

9 The troubles of an archbishop

While retaining the title of Archbishop of Canterbury, Edmund Grindal had been suspended from the exercise of his jurisdiction as early as 1577, when he refused to obey a royal order to suppress the prophesyings which the Queen regarded as a threat to traditional ecclesiastical discipline and even as the thin end of a wedge leading to Presbyterianism. This letter, written in 1583, shortly before Grindal's death makes it plain that he was preparing to resign his see, but, as it happens, on account of infirmity, not the Queen's wish.

It may please your lordship to be advertised that I have been loath of late to trouble your lordship with any suits, because I have been informed that you were very sickly. But trusting now that your lordship is in better case, and my time drawing on so fast, and also understanding by Doctor Aubrey that your lordship would have some notes of the value of this bishopric, I am bold to send the said Doctor Aubrey and my steward to inform your lordship of the state of the same, most instantly praying your good lordship to be a mean to her Majesty, both for proportioning my pension (wherein I doubt not her Majesty will have honourable consideration of my place, age and infirmities) and also to declare her Majesty's pleasure for order how the same may be answered unto me for the short time that I have to live. And as your lordship hath been, next unto her Majesty, the principal procurer of all my preferments, which I will acknowledge whilst I live with all thanksgiving, so I beseech you in this doing to be a mean to bring me to some hope of quietness in a private life, now in the end of my days, being now by age, sickness and infirmities not able to sustain the travails which apertain unto this great office. And by the grace of God I shall not fail, at the time heretofore appointed, to resign up my place in due form, for her Majesty's better satisfaction in that behalf. . . .

Grindal to Lord Burghley, 27 February 1583, in *The Remains of Edmund Grindal*, ed. W. Nicholson, Parker Soc. (1843), pp. 401–2

10   Exchange no robbery?

This act of Elizabeth's first parliament was designed to allow the Queen to plunder the Church. Its provisions—that she could exchange the lands of a vacant bishopric for impropriated tithes in her possession and that bishops should not be allowed to lease their lands for longer than three lives or 21 years except to the Crown—meant that Elizabeth was in fact able to take into her own hands a good deal of the best of the bishops' lands, which she then used to reward her courtiers and secular officials. This exploitation continued until the beginning of James I's reign when it was stopped by a statute of 1604, which forbade bishops to alienate the lands of their sees, even to the Crown.

The Lords Spiritual and Temporal and the Commons in this present parliament assembled, perceiving how necessary it is for the imperial crown of this realm to be repaired with restitution of revenues meet for the same, and having assented and fully accorded to restore to the same imperial crown the First Fruits and tenths and parsonages impropriate for the increase of the revenue thereof, be also desirous to devise some good means whereby the said revenue of tenths and impropriate benefices might be in the governance and disposition of the clergy of this realm, being most apt for the same, in such sort as yet thereby the said imperial crown should not be in any wise diminished in the said restored revenue; and therefore beseech your Majesty that it may be enacted by the authority of this present parliament in manner and form hereafter following; that is to say, upon the vacation and avoidance of every archbishopric or bishopric within this your realm of England and Wales and other your Highness' dominions, it shall and may be lawful for your Highness to elect and choose and to take into your hands and royal possession as much and so many of any the honours, castles, manors, lands, tenements, or other hereditaments, being parcel of the possessions of any such archbishopric or bishopric so being void, as the clear yearly value of all your Majesty's parsonages appropriate and yearly tenths within every such archbishopric or bishopric shall yearly amount and extend unto. . . . [And] it shall and may be lawful for your Highness by your letters patents to give and assure unto such archbishop and bishop and his successors as shall be preferred and consecrated archbishop or bishop of such archbishopric or bishopric so being void, so much and so many of your yearly tenths, tithes, and parsonages appropriated being within the same archbishopric or bishopric as shall be of as much or of more yearly value as the said honours, castles, manors, lands, tenements or hereditaments. . . .

And be it further enacted by the authority aforesaid, that all gifts, grants, feoffments, fines or other conveyance or estates from the first day of this present parliament to be had, made, done or suffered by any archbishop or bishop of any honours, castles, manors, lands, tenements or other hereditaments, being parcel of the possessions of his archbishopric or bishopric, or united, appertaining or belonging to any the same archbishoprics or bishoprics, to any person or persons, bodies politic or corporate (other than to the Queen's Highness her heirs or successors), whereby any estate or estates should or may pass from the same archbishops or bishops or any of them (other than for the term of 21 years or three lives from such time as any such lease, grant or assurance shall begin, and whereupon the old acustomed yearly rent or more shall be reserved and payable yearly during the said term of 21 years or three lives), shall be utterly void and of none effect. . . .

1 Eliz. c. 19, Statutes of the Realm, iv, 381–2

11   Clerical marriage

Although Elizabethan clergymen were allowed to marry, the Queen would personally have preferred a celibate clergy. Her injunctions of 1559 show a determination to ensure that ministers' wives should at least be suitable consorts. The provision that the consent of the woman's 'master or mistress' might be necessary is significant. It indicates the social class from which many clergymen's wives were expected to come, and is thus a commentary on the low social status of many of the priests of the time.

Item, although there be no prohibition by the word of God nor any example of the primitive church, but that the priests and ministers of the church may lawfully, for the avoiding of fornication, have an honest and sober wife, and that for the same purpose the same was by act of parliament in the time of our dear brother King Edward VI made lawful, whereupon a great number of the clergy of this realm were then married, and so yet continue. Yet because there hath grown offence and some slander to the church by lack of discreet and sober behaviour in many ministers of the church, both in choosing of their wives and indiscreet living with them, the remedy whereof is necessary to be sought, it is thought, therefore, very necessary that no manner of priest or deacon shall hereafter take to his wife any manner of woman without the advice and allowance first had upon good examination by the bishop of the same diocese, and two justices of the peace of the same shire, dwelling next to the place where the same woman hath made her most abode before her marriage, nor without the good will of the parents of the said woman, if she have any living, or two of the next of her kinsfolks, or, for lack of knowledge of such, of her master or mistress, where she serveth. And before he shall be contracted in any place, he shall make a good and certain proof thereof to the minister, or to the congregation assembled for that purpose, which shall be upon some holy day, where divers may be present. And if any shall do otherwise, that then they shall not be permitted to minister either the word or the sacraments of the church, nor shall be capable of any ecclesiastical benefice.

And for the manner of marriages of any bishops, the same shall be allowed and approved by the metropolitan of the province, and also by such commissioners as the Queen's Majesty shall thereunto appoint. And if any master or dean, or any head of any college, shall purpose to marry, the same shall not be allowed but by such to whom the visitation of the same doth properly belong, who shall in any wise provide that the same tend not to the hindrance of their house.

> The Injunctions of Queen Elizabeth, 1559, in *Documents Illustrative of English Church History*, ed. H. Gee and W. J. Hardy (1896), pp. 431–2

12   Back to the early Church

When the Elizabethan Church was established in 1559 it had to meet the charge —which came from Catholics and later on from Puritans as well—that it was merely a man-made institution with no theoretical justification from the Christian past. John Jewel was the first and, with the exception of Richard Hooker, the greatest Elizabethan to provide a philosophical justification for the Church. In his *Apology* of 1562 he defended it against Catholic criticisms by maintaining that, far from being just a temporal creation, it was a return to the true Church of the early Fathers, the pure form of Christianity which had been destroyed by the excesses of medieval Catholicism.

We are come, as near as we possibly could, to the church of the apostles and of the old catholic bishops and fathers, which church we know hath hitherunto been sound and perfect and, as Tertullian termeth it, a pure virgin, spotted as yet with no idolatry nor with any foul or shameful fault; and have directed according to their customs and ordinances not only our doctrine but also the sacraments and the form of common prayer.

And, as we know both Christ himself and all good men heretofore have done, we have called home again to the original and first foundation that religion which hath been foully neglected and utterly corrupted by these men. For we thought it meet thence to take the pattern of reforming religion from whence the ground of religion was first taken, because this one reason, as saith the most ancient father Tertullian, hath great force against all heresies: 'Look whatsoever was first, that is true; and whatsoever is latter, that is corrupt.' Irenaeus oftentimes appealed to the oldest churches, which had been nearest to Christ's time, and which it was hard to believe had erred. But why at this day is not the same common respect and consideration had? Why return we not to the pattern of the old churches? Why may not we hear at this time amongst us the same saying which was openly pronounced in times past in the council at Nicaea by so many bishops and catholic fathers and nobody once speaking against it . . . ; 'hold still the old customs?'

> John Jewel, *An Apology of the Church of England*, ed. J. E. Booty, Folger Shakespeare Library (Ithaca, 1963), pp. 121–2

13   The errors of the Puritans

The greatest defender of the Elizabethan Church was certainly Richard Hooker, a clergyman who never rose to high official position in the Church. Hooker published the first four books of his *Laws of Ecclesiastical Polity* in 1593. The work is a masterpiece of Elizabethan prose, as well as a theoretical study of the very first importance. In it Hooker provided a general justification for the position of the Church of England, but he was especially concerned to defend it against Puritan attacks, a task which he performed most effectively, as the following excerpts show.

The Second Book: concerning their first position who urge reformation in the Church of England, namely, that Scripture is the only rule of all things which in this life may be done by men.
. . . There is no necessity that if I confess I ought not to do that which the Scripture forbiddeth me, I should thereby acknowledge myself bound to do nothing which the Scripture commandeth me not. For many inducements besides Scripture may lead me to that which, if Scripture be against, they all give place and are of no value, yet otherwise are strong and effectual to persuade. . . .
The Third Book: concerning their second assertion, that in Scripture there must be of necessity contained a form of Church polity the laws whereof may in no wise be altered.
. . . Now as it can be to Nature no injury that of her we say the same which diligent beholders of her works have observed, namely that she provideth for all living creatures nourishment which may suffice, that she bringeth forth no kind of creature whereto she is wanting in that which is needful; although we do not so far magnify her exceeding bounty as to affirm that she bringeth into the world the sons of men adorned with gorgeous attire or maketh costly buildings to spring up out of the earth for them. So I trust that to mention what the Scripture of God leaveth unto the Church's discretion in some things is not in anything to impair the honour which the Church of God yieldeth

to the Sacred Scriptures' perfection. Wherein seeing that no more is by us maintained than only that Scripture must needs teach the Church whatsoever is in such sort necessary as hath been set down, and that it is no more disgrace for Scripture to have left a number of other things free to be ordered at the discretion of the Church than for Nature to have left it unto the wit of man to devise his own attire and not to look for it as the beasts of the field have theirs. . . .

. . . They which first gave out that nothing ought to be established in the Church which is not commanded by the Word of God, thought this principle plainly warranted by the manifest words of the Law. . . . Wherefore, having an eye to a number of rites and orders in the Church of England, as marrying with a ring, crossing in the one sacrament, kneeling at the other, observing of festival days more than only that which is called the Lord's Day, enjoining abstinence at certain times from some kinds of meat, churching of women after childbirth, degrees taken by divines in Universities, sundry Church offices, dignities and callings, for which they found no commandment in the Holy Scripture, they thought by the one only stroke of that axiom to have cut them off. But that which they took for an oracle, being sifted was repelled. . . .

. . . Sundry things may be lawfully done in the Church, so as they be not done against the Scripture, although no Scripture do command them, but the Church, only following the light of reason, judge them to be in discretion meet . . . , so that free and lawful it is to devise any ceremony, to receive any order, and to authorise any kind of regiment, no special commandment being thereby violated, and the same being thought such by them to whom the judgment thereof apperteineth, as that it is not scandalous but decent, tending unto edification, and setting forth the glory of God. . . .

The Fourth Book: concerning their third assertion, that our form of Church polity is corrupted with Popish orders, rites, and ceremonies, banished out of certain reformed Churches, whose example therein we ought to have followed.

. . . Concerning rites and ceremonies, there may be fault either in the kind or in the number and multitude of them. The first thing blamed about the kind of ours is that in many things we have departed from the ancient simplicity of Christ and his Apostles, we have embraced more outward stateliness, we have those orders in the exercise of religion which they who best pleased God and served him most devoutly never had. For it is out of doubt that the first state of things was best, that in the prime of the Christian religion faith was soundest, the

Scriptures of God were then best understood by all men, all parts of godliness did then most abound. . . . The glory of God and the good of his Church was the thing which the Apostles aimed at and therefore ought to be the mark whereat we also level. But seeing those rites and orders may be at one time more which at another time are less available unto that purpose, what reason is there in these things to urge the state of one only age as a pattern for all to follow? It is not, I am right sure, their meaning that we should now assemble our people to serve God in close and secret meetings; or that common brooks or rivers should be used for places of baptism; or that the Eucharist should be ministered after meat; or that the custom of Church-feasting should be renewed; or that all kinds of standing provision for the ministry should be utterly taken away and their estate made again dependent upon the voluntary devotion of men. In these things they easily perceive how unfit that were for the present, which was for the first age convenient enough. . . .

> R. Hooker, *Of the Laws of Ecclesiastical Polity*, in *The Works of Mr. Richard Hooker with an account of his life and death by Isaac Walton* (2 vols., Oxford, 1890), i, 249, 293, 294-5, 297-8, 351-3

14   Plans for a Presbyterian Church

When, after the vestiarian controversy of the 1560s, English Puritanism entered a more extreme phase in the 1570s, one of its principal targets was the institution of episcopacy. The radical Puritans, or Presbyterians, were under the leadership of Thomas Cartwright, who had been appointed Lady Margaret Professor of Divinity at Cambridge in 1569 but was deprived of his Chair in December 1570, because of his dangerous opinions. Cartwright was probably the author of the *Second Admonition to Parliament*, which was published in 1572. It worked out, admittedly in a somewhat confused way, a Presbyterian scheme of church government based on consistories made up of ministers and assistants (or elders as they were sometimes called) in each parish, conferences for convenient districts, and provincial and national synods. It also provided for popular election of ministers, and for deacons for the care of the poor—the latter office bearing witness to the advanced social conscience which was typical of many Puritans. This potentially revolutionary document led to a literary battle between Cartwright and John Whitgift, later archbishop of Canterbury, which continued for much of the 1570s.

. . . Next, you must repeal your statute or statutes whereby you have authorised that ministry that now is, making your estate partly to consist of Lords spiritual (as you call them), and making one minister higher than another, appointing also an order to ordain ministers, which order is clean differing from the Scriptures; wherefore you must have the order for these things drawn out of the Scriptures, which order is this. When any parish is destitute of a pastor or of a teacher, the same parish may have recourse to the next conference, and to them make it known, that they may procure chiefly from the one of the universities, or, if otherwise, a man learned and of good report, whom, after trial of his gifts had in their conference, they may present unto the parish which before had been with them about that matter, but yet so that the same parish have him a certain time amongst them, that they may be acquainted with his gifts and behaviour and give their consents for his stay amongst them if they can allege no just cause to the contrary; for he may not be sent away again which is so sent to a parish except a just cause of misliking, the cause alleged being justly proved against him either amongst themselves in their own consistory, so that he will appeal no further for his trial, or else in the next conference, or council provincial, or national, unto which from one to another he may appeal . . . ; and if he give over they may proceed as afore for another. And when such an one is found to whom the parish must give consent because there is no just cause to be alleged against him, the next conference by whose means he was procured shall be certified of the parish's liking, whereupon they shall amongst themselves agree upon one of the ministers which shall be sent by them to the same parish, and after a sermon made according to the occasion, and earnest prayer to God, with fasting according to the example of the Scriptures, made by that congregation to God that it would please him to direct them in their choice and to bless that man whom they choose, he shall require to know their consent, which being granted he and the elders shall lay their hands on him, to signify to him that he is lawfully called to that parish to be pastor there or teacher. . . .

. . . This is the right way to bring the ministry into credit and estimation—their gifts given them of God and their painfulness and honest life amongst their congregations, and not to make some of them Lords, Graces, Earls, Prelate and Register of the Garter, Barons, Suffragans, some of them rich Deans, Archdeacons, Masters of Colleges, Chancellors, Prebends, rich parsons and vicars, and though some of them be poor enough to get them credit by their rochets, hoods, caps, cloaks, tippets, and gowns, or such-like implements used by the Pharisees, which claimed high rooms and made large borders on their garments, and loved to be greeted and to be called

Rabbi, which things by our Saviour are forbidden his ministers and an order enjoined that they which look for it should not have it but be least esteemed. . . .

. . . I have already made mention of a consistory which were to be had in every congregation. That consisteth first of the ministers of the same congregation, as the guides and mouth of the rest, to direct them by the Scriptures, and to speak at their appointment that which shall be contested upon amongst them all, because of their gifts and place amongst them, which maketh them more fit for those purposes. The assistants are they whom the parish shall consent upon and choose for their good judgment in religion and godliness . . . , using the advice of their ministers therein chiefly . . . and also using earnest prayers with fasting, as in the choice of the minister; and having made their choice, thereafter they shall publish their agreement in their parish, and, after a sermon by their minister, at their appointment and upon their consent the minister may lay his hands upon every of them to testify to them their admission. . . . This consistory . . . shall examine all disordered ceremonies used in place of prayer and abolish those which they find evil or unprofitable, and bring in such orders as their congregation shall have need of, so they be few and apparent, necessary both for edifying and profit and decent order, proving it plainly to the whole Church that it is so. . . . These shall receive the informations of the deacons for the relief of the poor and their accounts for that which they shall lay out that way and of their diligence in visiting them, that the congregations may by the consistory be certified of all things concerning the poor, both that there may be made provision accordingly, and that the provision made may be well husbanded, and the poor may by the deacons be visited, comforted, and relieved according to their lack. Lastly, one or more of these assistants, with one of the ministers and a deacon or deacons, shall be those that shall at their Church's charges meet at the provincial council, or national, if there be any business that concerneth their Church. . . . A deacon is an officer of the Church for the behoof of the poor, chosen to this office by the congregation by such means as afore is prescribed in the choice of elders, by advice and consent, being a noted man for godly judgment and faithfulness. . . .

The Second Admonition to Parliament, 1572,
in J. R. Tanner, *Tudor Constitutional Documents* (2nd ed., 1930), pp. 167–70

15   The Queen rebuked!

This letter, in which Archbishop Grindal informed the Queen of his refusal to suppress the prophesyings which she disliked so much, is, because of its forthright tone, one of the most courageous documents ever sent by a subject to a Tudor monarch. It led to Grindal's suspension from all his archiepiscopal functions. The fact that an archbishop could emerge as a staunch defender of what the Queen regarded as essentially Puritan exercises illustrates the dangers and difficulties of applying words like Anglican and Puritan *tout court* to the more moderate individual members of the Elizabethan Church.

With most humble remembrance of my bounden duty to your Majesty. It may please the same to be advertised that the speeches which it hath pleased you to deliver unto me when I last attended on your Highness, concerning abridging the number of preachers and the utter suppression of all learned exercises and conferences among the ministers of the church, allowed by their bishops and ordinaries, have exceedingly dismayed and discomforted me. Not so much for that the said speeches sounded very hardly against mine own person, being but one particular man, and not much to be accounted of, but most of all for that the same might both tend to the public harm of God's church, whereof your Highness ought to be *nutricia*, and also to the heavy burdening of your own conscience before God, if they should be put in strict execution. It was not your Majesty's pleasure then, the time not serving thereto, to hear me at any length concerning the said two matters then propounded. I thought it therefore my duty by writing to declare some part of my mind unto your Highness. . . .

And so, to come to the present case . . . surely I cannot marvel enough how this strange opinion should once enter into your mind that it should be good for the church to have few preachers.

Alas, Madam! is the scripture more plain in any one thing than that the gospel of Christ should be plentifully preached and that plenty of labourers should be sent into the Lord's harvest, which, being great and large, standeth in need not of a few but many workmen? . . .

Public and continual preaching of God's word is the ordinary mean and instrument of the salvation of mankind. St. Paul calleth it the ministry of reconciliation of man unto God. By preaching of God's word the glory of God is enlarged, faith is nourished, and charity increased. By it the ignorant is instructed, the negligent exhorted and incited, the stubborn rebuked, the weak conscience comforted, and to all those that sin of malicious wickedness the wrath of God is threatened. By preaching also due obedience to Christian princes and magistrates is planted in the hearts of subjects: for obedience proceedeth of conscience; conscience is grounded upon the word of God; the word of God worketh his effect by preaching. So as generally, where preaching wanteth, obedience faileth. . . .

Now for the second point, which is concerning the learned exercise and conference amongst the ministers of the church: I have consulted with divers of my brethren, the bishops, by letters; who think the same as I do, viz. a thing profitable to the church, and therefore expedient to be continued. . . .

I trust, when your Majesty hath considered and well weighed the premises you will rest satisfied and judge that no such inconveniences can grow of these exercises as you have been informed, but rather the clean contrary. And for my own part, because I am very well assured, both by reasons and arguments taken out of the holy scriptures, and by experience (the most certain seal of sure knowledge), that the said exercises, for the interpretation and exposition of the scriptures, and for exhortation and comfort drawn out of the same, are both profitable to increase knowledge among the ministers, and tendeth to the edifying of the hearers—I am forced, with all humility, and yet plainly, to profess that I cannot with safe conscience and without the offence of the Majesty of God give my assent to the suppressing of the said exercises: much less can I send out any injunction for the utter and universal subversion of the same. . . .

If it be your Majesty's pleasure, for this or any other cause, to remove me out of this place, I will with all humility yield thereunto and render again to your Majesty that I received of the same. . . .

Bear with me, I beseech you, Madam, if I choose rather to offend your earthly majesty than to offend the heavenly majesty of God. And now, being sorry that I have been so long and tedious to your Majesty I will draw to an end, most humbly praying the same well to consider these two short petitions following.

The first is that you would refer all these ecclesiastical matters which touch religion, or the doctrine and discipline of the church, unto the bishops and divines of your realm, according to the example of all godly Christian emperors and princes of all ages. For indeed they are things to be judged (as an ancient father writeth), *in ecclesia, seu synodo, non in palatio*. When your Majesty hath questions of the laws of your realm, you do not decide the same in your Court, but send them to your judges to be determined. Likewise, for doubts in matters of doctrine or discipline of the church, the ordinary way is to refer the decision of the same to the bishops and other head ministers of the church. . . .

The second petition I have to make to your Majesty is this: that, when you deal in matters of faith and religion, or matters that touch the church of Christ, which is his spouse, bought with so dear a price, you would not use to pronounce so resolutely and peremptorily, *quasi ex auctoritate*, as ye may do in civil and extern matters, but always remember that in God's causes the will of God and not the will of any earthly creature is to take place. It is the antichristian voice of the Pope, *Sic volo, sic jubeo; stet pro ratione voluntas*. . . .

Remember, Madam, that you are a mortal creature. 'Look not only (as was said to Theodosius) upon the purple and princely array, wherewith ye are apparelled, but consider withal what is that that is covered therewith. Is it not flesh and blood? Is it not dust and ashes? Is it not a corruptible body, which must return to his earth again, God knoweth how soon?' . . .

And although ye are a mighty prince, yet remember that He which dwelleth in heaven is mightier. . . .

Wherefore, I do beseech you Madam . . . , when you deal in these religious causes, set the majesty of God before your eyes, laying all earthly majesty aside: determine with yourself to obey His voice, and with all humility say unto Him, *Non mea, sed tua voluntas fiat*. God hath blessed you with great felicity in your reign, now many years. Beware you do not impute the same to your own deserts or policy, but give God the glory. And as to instruments and means, impute your said felicity, first, to the goodness of the cause which ye have set forth (I mean Christ's true religion) and, secondly, to the sighs and groanings of the godly in their fervent prayer to God for you, which have hitherto, as it were, tied and bound the hands of God that He could not pour out His plagues upon you and your people, most justly deserved.

> Archbishop Grindal to the Queen, December
> 1576, *The Remains of Edmund Grindal*, ed.
> W. Nicholson, Parker Soc. (1843), pp. 376–90

16 Whitgift's three articles

John Whitgift, who succeeded the disgraced Grindal at Canterbury in 1583, was prepared to take decisive action against the Puritans. Soon after his appointment he demanded subscription from the clergy to the three articles printed below. Puritans could accept the first, and some of them possibly also the third, but the demand that they should agree that the Prayer Book contained 'nothing in it contrary to the word of God' was highly offensive to the consciences of even the more moderate Puritans. Whitgift's struggle to secure the deprivation of those ministers who refused to subscribe was opposed by powerful forces at Court, including many prominent privy councillors (see Document 19), and he had to be content in the end with a modified form of subscription which most Puritans could accept. By the end of 1584, when the immediate crisis was over, very few Puritan ministers had been deprived. Whitgift, however, by no means abandoned his efforts to secure uniformity and in the much more favourable atmosphere of the late 1580s and early 1590s he was able to use the High Commission and Star Chamber to crush organised Presbyterianism in the Church.

6. That none be permitted to preach, read, catechize, minister the sacraments, or to execute any other ecclesiastical function, by what authority soever he be admitted thereunto, unless he consent and subscribe to these Articles following, before the ordinary of the diocese wherein he preacheth, readeth, catechizeth, or ministereth the sacraments, viz.:

(1) That her Majesty, under God, hath, and ought to have, the sovereignty and rule over all manner of persons born within her realms, dominions, and countries, of what estate, either ecclesiastical or temporal, soever they be; and that no foreign power, prelate, state, or potentate hath, or ought to have, any jurisdiction, power, superiority, pre-eminence or authority, ecclesiastical or spiritual, within her Majesty's said realms, dominions and countries.

(2) That the Book of Common Prayer, and of ordering bishops, priests, and deacons, containeth nothing in it contrary to the word of God, and that the same may lawfully be used, and that he himself will use the form of the said book prescribed in public prayer and adminis-tration of the sacraments, and none other.

(3) That he alloweth the book of Articles of religion, agreed upon by the archbishops and bishops of both provinces, and the whole clergy in the Convocation holden at London in the year of our Lord God 1562, and set forth by her Majesty's authority, and that he believeth all the Articles therein contained to be agreeable to the word of God.

> Articles touching preachers, and other orders for the Church, 1583, *Documents Illustrative of English Church History*, ed. H. Gee and W. J. Hardy (1896), p. 482

17   A day in the life of a Puritan lady

This entry is typical of many which appear in the diary of Lady Margaret Hoby, a Yorkshire heiress totally committed to the Puritan movement, as was her third husband, Sir Thomas Posthumus Hoby. His name does not appear in this excerpt, but occurs frequently elsewhere in the diary. Mr. Rhodes seems to have been her domestic chaplain. In Lady Hoby's case extreme piety was clearly accompanied by a severe guilt complex, and the whole diary would provide a field day for a group of academic psychologists.

In the morning after private prayers and order taken for dinner I wrote some notes in my Testament till 10 o'clock; then I went to walk and, after I returned home, I prayed privately, read a chapter of the Bible, and wrought [i.e. embroidered] till dinner time. After, I walked awhile with Mr Rhodes and then I wrought and did some things about the house till 4. Then I wrote out the sermon into my book preached the day before and, when I had again gone about in the house and given order for supper and other things, I returned to examination and prayer. Then I walked till supper time and, after catechising, meditated awhile of that I had heard, with mourning to God for pardon both of my omission and commission wherein I found myself guilty, I went to bed.

Diary of Lady Margaret Hoby, 1599–1605, ed.
Dorothy M. Meads (1930), pp. 62–3

18   A Puritan sermon

This sermon, by 'silver-tongued' Henry Smith, a notable Puritan divine, gives some idea of the vigour of Elizabethan preaching. Even modern readers can almost suffer with the sinner, and the effects of such sermons on the minds of contemporaries who had often active physical fears of the realities of Hell can be better imagined than described.

(In this passage contemporary spelling has been retained in order to give the full flavour of the original.)

If there be any hell in this world, they which feel the Worme of conscience gnaw upon their hearts, may truly say, that they have felt the torments of hell. Who can expresse that man's horror but himselfe? Sorrowes are met in his soule at a feast: and fear, thought, and anguish divide his soule between them. All the furies of hell leaps upon his heart like a stage. Thought calleth to Fear; Fear whistleth to Horrour;

Horrour beckoneth to Despair, and saith, Come and help me to torment the sinner: One saith, that she cometh from this sinne, and
another saith, that she cometh from that sinne: so he goeth thorow a
thousand deaths, and cannot die. Irons are laid upon his body like a
prisoner. All his lights are put out at once: he hath no soul fit to be
comforted. Thus he lies upon the racke, and saith that he beares the
world upon his shoulders, and that no man suffereth that which he
suffereth. So let him lye (saith God) without ease, untill he confesse and
repent, and call for mercie. This is the godly way which the Serpent
said would make you Gods, and made him a Devill.

Cited in W. Haller, *The Rise of Puritanism*
(New York, 1938), pp. 33–4

19   Patronage for the Puritans

The importance of patronage was all-pervasive in the Elizabethan Church and
state and this letter from the Queen's favourite, the Earl of Leicester, to a
Puritan preacher who had rebuked him gives some idea of the great influence
which he wielded in filling important Church offices. Leicester was the most
influential of all the really committed defenders of Puritanism during Elizabeth's
reign and his death in 1588 was a most serious blow to the Puritan party in the
Church. It was the removal of Leicester's influence in the Privy Council and in
the country at large rather than the defeat of the Armada which cleared the way
for Whitgift's successful assault on the organised Presbyterian movement in the
early 1590s. (For another aspect of this discussion see III, 12.)

. . . As for me to be thought an enemy so soon to God's church, I dare
thus far vaunt of myself, and the rather being a just and good cause I
may well do it: that there is no man I know in this realm of one calling
or other that hath showed a better mind to the furthering of true
religion than I have done, even from the first day of her Majesty's
reign to this. And when times of some trouble hath been among the
preachers and ministers of the church for matters of ceremonies and
such like, knowing many of them to be hardly handled for so small
causes, who did move for them, both at the bishops' hands and at the
prince's? Or who in England had more blame of both for the success
that followed thereby than myself? I would fain know at the most
devilish enemy's hand that I have what one act have I done to hinder
or diminish the church of God since the beginning of this time to this
day? I defy their worst. For my conscience doth witness the contrary.
And for proof of it, look of all the bishops that can be supposed that I
have commended to that dignity since my credit any way served, and

look whether they were not men as well thought of as any among the clergy before. Look of all the deans that in that time also have been commended by me. Look into the university of Oxford likewise, whereof I am chancellor and see what heads of houses be there now in comparison of those I found. And do but indifferently examine how the ministry is advanced there, even where were not long ago not only many ill heads but as many the worst and untoward scholars for religion. Beside this, who in England hath had or hath more learned chaplains belonging to him than I, or hath preferred more to the furtherance of the church of learned preachers? Or what bishop (since I must now speak for myself) in England beside the number of preachers that I countenance of mine own, doth give so large stipends out of his purse to them as I do? And where have I refused any one preacher or good minister to do for him the best I could at all times, when they have need of me either to speak or write for them? . . .

> The Earl of Leicester to Thomas Wood, 19 August 1576, in *Letters of Thomas Wood, Puritan, 1566–67*, ed. P. Collinson (Bulletin of the Institute of Historical Research, Special Supplement, No. 5, 1960), p. 13

20 The Queen deposed

Before the issue of Pius V's Bull of deposition against the Queen in 1570, Elizabeth had treated English Catholics with a good deal of leniency, her hope being that Catholicism would gradually die out and its suppporters be assimilated to a Church of England which preserved enough of the old Church's organisation and ritual to be acceptable to them. The Bull brought this tacit truce to an end. Whatever its moral claims, it failed disastrously at the time of its coming, for it shared in the ignominy of the collapse of the Rising of the North, whose triumph it was to have stimulated and sanctified.

Pius Bishop, servant to God's servants, for a future memorial of the matter.

He that reigneth on high, to whom is given all power in Heaven and in Earth, hath committed his One, Holy, Catholic and Apostolic Church, out of which there is no salvation, to one alone upon earth, namely to Peter the chief of the Apostles, and to Peter's successor the Bishop of Rome, to be by him governed with plenary authority. Him alone hath he made prince over all people and all kingdoms, to pluck up, destroy, scatter, consume, plant, and build; that he may preserve his faithful people (knit together with the band of charity) in the unity of the Spirit, and present them spotless and unblameable to their Saviour. In discharge of which function, We, who are by God's goodness called to the government of the aforesaid Church, do spare no pains, labouring with all earnestness that unity and the Catholic Religion (which the Author thereof hath, for the trial of his children's faith and for our amendment, suffered to be tossed with so great afflictions) might be preserved sincere. But the number of the ungodly hath gotten such power that there is now no place in the whole world left which they have not essayed to corrupt with their most wicked doctrines; and amongst others, Elizabeth, the pretended Queen of England, the servant of wickedness, lendeth thereunto her helping hand, with whom, as in a sanctuary, the most pernicious persons have found a refuge. This very woman, having seized on the kingdom and monstrously usurped the place of Supreme Head of the Church in all England and the chief authority and jurisdiction thereof, hath again reduced the said kingdom into a miserable and ruinous condition, which was so lately reclaimed to the Catholic faith and a thriving condition. . . .

. . . We seeing that impieties and wicked actions are multiplied one upon another, as also that the persecution of the faithful and affliction for religion groweth every day heavier and heavier, through the instigation and by means of the said Elizabeth, and since We understand her heart to be so hardened and obdurate that she hath not only contemned the godly requests and admonitions of Catholic princes concerning her cure and conversion but also hath not so much as suffered the nuncios of this See to cross the seas for this purpose into England, are constrained of necessity to betake ourselves to the weapons of justice against her, being heartily grieved and sorry that we are compelled thus to punish one to whose ancestors the whole state of Christendom hath been so much beholden. Being therefore supported with His authority whose pleasure it was to place Us (though unable for so great a burden) in this Supreme Throne of Justice, We do out of the fullness of Our Apostolic power declare the aforesaid Elizabeth as being an heretic and a favourer of heretics, and her adherents in the matters aforesaid, to have incurred the sentence of excommunication, and to be cut off from the unity of the Body of Christ. And moreover We do declare her to be deprived of her pretended title to the kingdom aforesaid, and of all dominion, dignity, and privilege whatsoever; and also the nobility, subjects, and people of the said kingdom, and all others who have in any sort sworn unto her, to be for ever absolved from any such oath, and all manner of duty of dominion, allegiance, and obedience: and We also do by authority of these presents absolve them, and do deprive the said Elizabeth of her pretended title to the kingdom, and all other things before named. And We do command and charge all and every the noblemen, subjects, people, and others aforesaid that they presume not to obey her or her orders, mandates and laws; and those which shall do the contrary We do include them in the like sentence of anathema. . . .

The Papal Bull, *Regnans in Excelsis*, 1570, W. Camden, *Elizabeth* (4th ed., 1688), pp. 146-7

21 Catholicism and treason: Burghley's defence of his policy

The threat posed to the Queen's and England's security by the issue of the Bull of deposition in 1570 and by the arrival of seminary priests and Jesuits in England in the 1570s and 1580s led to the issue of penal laws by which Catholics could be executed as traitors. William Cecil, in his *Execution of Justice*, first published in 1583, set out the English government's view of the position: namely, that those executed suffered not because of their religion, but because they refused allegiance to the Crown in temporal matters. In considering such tolerance as existed in practice however, it must be borne in mind that, since priests and the Mass were prohibited, the survival of Catholicism was clearly and deliberately opposed.

And though there are many subjects known in the realm that differ in some opinions of religion from the Church of England and that do also not forbear to profess the same, yet in that they do also profess loyalty and obedience to Her Majesty and offer readily in Her Majesty's defence to impugn and resist any foreign force, though it should come or be procured from the Pope himself, none of these sort are for their contrary opinions in religion prosecuted or charged with any crimes or pains of treason, nor yet willingly searched in their consciences for their contrary opinions that savour not of treason. And of these sorts there [have been and] are a number of persons, not of such base and vulgar note as those were which of late have been executed, as in particular some by name are well known and not unfit to be remembered.

The first and chiefest by office was Dr. Heath, that was Archbishop of York and Lord Chancellor of England in Queen Mary's time, who at the first coming of Her Majesty to the crown, showing himself a faithful and quiet subject, continued in both the said offices, though in religion then manifestly differing, and yet was he not restrained of his liberty nor deprived of his proper lands and goods, but, leaving willingly both his offices, lived in his own house very discreetly and enjoyed all his purchased lands during his natural life, until by very age he departed this world and then left his house and living to his friends, an example of gentleness never matched in Queen Mary's time.

> *The Execution of Justice in England and A True,*
> *Sincere and Modest Defense of English Catholics,*
> ed. R. M. Kingdon, Folger Shakespeare
> Library (Ithaca, 1965), pp. 9–10

22   The Catholics defended: Cardinal Allen's pamphlet

William Allen's *Defense of the English Catholics*, published in 1584, was a reply by the foremost English Catholic of the day to Cecil's *Execution of Justice*. Allen, as was to be expected, took precisely the opposite line from Cecil. According to him Catholics were being persecuted and executed for their religion. He was certainly right, given his premises, but so, of course, was Cecil. At a time when politics and religion were inextricably tied together the Elizabethan Catholics were both martyrs and traitors at the same time. Certainly, Allen himself gave full support to the Spanish Armada of 1588 which was directed to depose the English queen by force.

The truth is that in the first year and Parliament of the Queen's reign, when they abolished the Pope's authority and would have yielded the same authority with the title of supreme head to the Queen as it was given before to her father and brother, divers specially moved by minister Calvin's writing (who had condemned in the same princes that calling), liked not the term and therefore procured that some other equivalent but less offensive might be used. Upon which formality, it was enacted that she was 'the chief governor as well in causes ecclesiastical or spiritual as civil and temporal'. And an oath of the same was conceived accordingly, to be tendered at their pleasures to all the spiritual and temporal officers in the realm, by which every one must swear that in conscience he taketh and believeth her so to be, and that no priest or other born out of the realm can have or ought to have any manner of power in spiritual matters over her subjects. Which oath is counted the very torment of all English consciences, not the Protestants themselves believing it to be true. And of all true Catholics, as before it was deemed in her father, a layman, and in her brother, a child, very ridiculous, so now in herself, being a woman, is it accounted a thing most monstrous and unnatural and the very gap to bring any realm to the thralldom of all sects, heresy, paganism, Turkism, or atheism that the prince for the time by human frailty may be subject unto, all our religion, faith, worship, service, and prayers depending upon his sovereign determination, a thing that all nations have to take heed of by our example, for the redress of which pernicious absurdity so many of our said brethren so willingly have shed their blood. . . .

See whether a portable altar be a sufficient cause to give the torture to a grave, worshipful person, not so much as suspected of treason or any disobedience, other than in cases of conscience. Whether books of prayers and meditations spiritual, or the printing and spreading of them, be a rack matter in any commonwealth Christian. Look whether your ordinary demands were of that weight and quality as were to be answered by constraint of the rack. Let the world see what one confession of treasonable matter you have wrested out by the so often tormenting of so many, and what great secrecies touching the state (which you pretend so earnestly to seek for) you have found amongst them all. No, no, nothing was there in those religious hearts but innocency and true religion. It is that which you punished, tormented, and deadly hated in them. If they would have in the least point in the world condescended to your desires in that, or but once for your pleasures presented themselves at your schismatical prayers, all racking and treasons had been cleared and past.

> *The Execution of Justice in England and A True,*
> *Sincere and Modest Defense of English Catholics,*
> ed. R. M. Kingdon, Folger Shakespeare Library
> (Ithaca, 1965), pp. 67–8, 73–4

23 The faith of a martyr

This account by the Jesuit Edmund Campion of his reasons for coming to England in 1580, written at the beginning of his mission, bears witness to the transparent sincerity which impressed almost everybody who met him. The devotion and dedication of the Catholic priests—the seculars as well as the Jesuits—who entered England from the 1570s onwards help to explain the impression which they made on the minds of those Englishmen whom they sustained in, or converted to, the Catholic faith. Many of these priests were martyred like Campion himself, who was executed in December 1581.

. . . touching our society, be it known to you that we have made a league . . . cheerfully to carry the cross you shall lay upon us, and never to despair of your recovery, while we have a man left to enjoy your Tyburn, or to be wracked with your torments, or consumed with your prisons. The expense is reckoned, the enterprise is begun; it is of God, it cannot be withstood. So the faith was planted, so it must be restored.

P. McGrath, *Papists and Puritans under Elizabeth I* (1967), pp. 168–9

24   A parish at worship

It is important to contrast the fervour of Puritan and Catholic enthusiasts and the devoutness of the best divines of the Church of England—the attitude, that is to say, of the Cartwrights, Campions and Hookers of the Elizabethan age—with the highly conventional devotion of those described in the following passage. These parishioners, largely indifferent to religion in any deeper sense of the word, may have been typical of a substantial section of the population.

And for my parishioners, they are a kind of people that love a pot of ale better than a pulpit, and a corn-rick better than a church-door, who, coming to divine service more for fashion that devotion, are contented after a little capping and kneeling, coughing and spitting, to help me to sing out a psalm, and sleep at the second lesson, or awake to stand up at the gospel, and say 'Amen' at the peace of God, and stay till the banns of matrimony be asked, or till the clerk have cried a pied stray bullock, a black sheep or a gray mare, and then, for that some dwell far off, be glad to be gotten home to dinner.

Nicolas Breton, 'A merrie dialogue betwixt the taker and mistaker' (1603), in A. Nicoll, *The Elizabethans* (Cambridge, 1957), p. 53, no. 132

25   Sir Walter Raleigh doubts

There were a few genuine sceptics among Elizabethan Englishmen, like Sir Walter Raleigh, whose doubts about the soul make interesting reading. Raleigh's scepticism probably did not extend as far as the atheism of which he was often accused, but reports of the following conversation, which reached official circles, produced enough alarm there to lead to a full scale investigation.

Rev. Ralph Ironside, Minister of Winterbotham:
Towards the end of supper some loose speeches of Mr. Carew Raleigh's being gently reproved by Sir Ralph Horsey in these words, '*Colloquia prava corrumpunt bones* [sic.] *mores* [Evil words corrupt good morals],' Mr. Raleigh demands of me what danger he might incur by such speeches.

Whereunto I answered: 'The wages of sin is death.'

And he making light of death as being common to all, sinner and righteous, I inferred further that as that life which is the gift of God through Jesus Christ is life eternal, so that death which is properly the wages of sin is death eternal, both of the body and of the soul also.

'Soul!' quoth Mr. Carew Raleigh, 'what is that?'

'Better it were,' said I, 'that we would be careful how the souls might be saved than to be curious in finding out their essence.'

And so keeping silence, Sir Walter requests me that for their instruction I would answer to the question that before by his brother was proposed unto me.

'I have been,' said he, 'a scholar some time in Oxford, I have answered under a Bachelor of Arts, and had talk with divers, yet hitherunto in this point (to wit, what the reasonable soul of man is) have I not by any been resolved. They tell us it is *primus motor*, the first mover, in a man, etc.'

Unto this, after I had replied that howsoever the soul were *fons et principium*, the fountain, beginning and cause of motion in us, yet the first mover was the brain or heart.

I was again urged to show my opinion, and hearing Sir Walter tell of his dispute and scholarship some time in Oxford, I cited the general definition of *anima* out of Aristotle 2 *de Anima* cap. I . . .

. . . It was misliked of Sir Walter as obscure and intricate. And I withal yielded that though it could not unto him, as being learned, yet it might seem obscure to the most present, and therefore had rather say with divines plainly that the reasonable soul is a spiritual and immortal substance breathed into man by God, whereby he lives and moves and understandeth, and so is distinguished from other creatures.

'Yes, but what is that spiritual and immortal substance breathed into man, etc.?' saith Sir Walter.

'The soul,' quoth I.

'Nay, then,' saith he, 'you answer not like a scholar.'

Cited in N. L. Williams, *Sir Walter Raleigh*
(Penguin ed., 1965), pp. 133–4

V

GOVERNMENT AND ADMINISTRATION

1 The divine foundations of government

The first book of Homilies, designed to be read in churches for popular edification, was published in 1547, just after Edward VI's accession to the throne, and Elizabeth ordered it to be reprinted in the early years of her reign. The homily of obedience set out clearly the divine sanction behind the existing political and social order. It thus both justified and reflected the contemporary axiom that the Queen had, by God's authority, the right to issue commands to her people, and that subjects had a duty to obey or at the very least not to resist such orders. Our second extract indicates the material weakness beneath the grandiose titles.

Almighty God hath created and appointed all things in heaven, earth, and waters, in a most excellent and perfect order. In heaven He hath appointed distinct and several orders and states of Archangels and Angels. In earth He hath assigned and appointed Kings, Princes, with other Governors under them, in all good and necessary order. . . . And man himself also hath all his parts both within and without, as soul, heart, mind, memory, understanding, reason, speech, with all and singular corporal members of his body in a profitable, necessary and pleasant order. Every degree of people in their vocation, calling and office hath appointed to them their duty and order: some are in high degree, some in low, some Kings and Princes, some inferiors and subjects, priests and laymen, masters and servants, fathers and children, husbands and wives, rich and poor: and everyone hath need of other: so that in all things is to be lauded and praised the goodly order of God; without the which no house, no city, no commonwealth, can continue and endure, or last. For, where there is no right order, there reigneth all abuse, carnal liberty, enormity, sin, and Babylonical confusion. Take away Kings, Princes, rulers, magistrates, judges and such estates of God's order; no man shall ride or go by the highway unrobbed; no man shall sleep in his own house or bed unkilled; no man shall keep his wife, children and possessions in quietness: all things shall be common: and there must needs follow all mischief and utter destruction both of souls, bodies, goods, and commonwealths.

But blessed be God that we in this realm of England feel not the horrible calamities, miseries and wretchedness which all they undoubtedly feel and suffer that lack this godly order: and praised be God that we know the great excellent benefit of God showed towards us in this behalf.

> The homily of Obedience, *Sermons or homilies appointed to be read in churches in the time of Queen Elizabeth* (1817), pp. 95–6

2 Thoughts about France

John Stubbes wrote his *Gaping Gulf* in 1579 to draw attention to the dangers which he saw in the proposed marriage between Elizabeth and the Duke of Alencon, heir to the French throne. By publishing such a tract Stubbs committed the grave crime of meddling with 'matters of state'. The Queen may not have been serious in considering the match—historians cannot be sure—but she reacted with fury to Stubbes's outburst and he was sentenced to have his right hand cut off. This savage penalty reflected the Queen's determination to defend her prerogative, in this case reflected in her marriage and her foreign policy.

There is another dangerous danger in this foreign French match that ariseth yet far higher, in that he is the brother of childless France. So as, if Henry the Third, now King, should die the morrow after our marriage, and Monsieur repair home, as we may be sure he would, into his native country, a larger and better kingdom, then, by all likelihood, either must our Elizabeth go with him out of her own native country and sweet soil of England, where she is Queen as possessor and inheritor of this imperial crown with all regal rights, dignities, prerogatives, pre-eminences, privileges, authorities, and jurisdictions of this kingly office and having the kingrich in her own person, into a foreign kingdom where her writ doth not run and shall be but in a borrowed majesty as the moon to the sun, shining by night as other kings' wives, and so she that hath ruled all this while here shall be there overruled in a strange land by some beldame, not without awe perhaps of a sister-in-law, and we her poor subjects that have been governed hitherto by a natural mother shall be overlooked at home by some cruel and proud governor, or else must she tarry here without comfort of her husband, seeing herself despised or not wifelike esteemed and as an eclipsed sun diminished in sovereignty, having such perhaps appointed to serve her and be at her commandment, after the French phrase, which in plain English will govern her and her state.

> L. E. Berry, *John Stubbes's Gaping Gulf and Letters and other relevant documents*, Folger Shakespeare Library (Charlottesville, Virginia, 1968), pp. 48–9

3   The Queen in Council

This passage is further evidence of the Queen following a policy to which her whole council of ministers had expressed opposition. On this occasion, in the summer of 1562, she was prepared to meet Mary, Queen of Scots, against the unanimous opinion of her leading advisers. She later on reversed this decision but that was due to changed political circumstances rather than to second thoughts about the advisability of following a unanimous recommendation of the Privy Council.

Lethington arrived since his last despatch with letters of earnest desire from his mistress [Mary Queen of Scots] of the interview, which since he has diligently solicited, and thereby brought the Queen in such a liking of the same, as, albeit at a full Council (the Queen being present, and the matter objected against by each councillor), she answered them all with such fineness of wit and excellence of utterance as for the same she was commended; and not allowing replication she concluded that if she had not such advertisement from Throckmorton that justly might cause her to stay, go she would. It is both groaned at and lamented of the most and wisest. . . .

> Sir Henry Sidney to Sir Nicholas Throckmorton, ambassador to France, 14 June 1562, *Cal. S.P. Foreign 1562*, p. 93

4   The Privy Council in the dark

Though Leicester held the highest office in the Netherlands, he appears to have been kept in the dark about high politics in the spring of 1586, when Elizabeth kept the question of English policy in the Netherlands in her own hands.

. . . I have let my lords [of the Privy Council] here understand how unkindly your lordship taketh it that you hear so seldom from them and that since your charge there you never received any letter of advice from them. They answer, as it is truth, that, her Majesty retaining the whole direction of the causes of that country to herself and such advice as she receiveth underhand, they know not what to write or to advise.

Sir Francis Walsingham to the Earl of Leicester, 25 April 1586, *Leycester Correspondence*, ed. J. Bruce, *Camden Soc.*, xxvii (1844), p. 237

5 The words of a statesman

Burghley's letter on the duties of a minister can be taken as a classic Elizabethan statement on the subject. He was, however, the most sophisticated English statesman of his age; and his subtle and complex influence over the queen was greater than he would ever acknowledge.

. . . I do hold, and will always, this course in such matters as I differ in opinion from her Majesty; as long as I may be allowed to give advice I will not change my opinion by affirming the contrary, for that were to offend God, to whom I am sworn first; but as a servant I will obey her Majesty's commandment and no wise contrary the same, presuming that she being God's chief minister here, it shall be God's will to have her commandments obeyed, after that I have performed my duty as a councillor, and shall in my heart wish her commandments to have such good successes as I am sure she intendeth. . . .

Lord Burghley to Sir Robert Cecil, 23 March 1596, *Queen Elizabeth and her times*, ed. T. Wright ii (1838), p. 457

6 Divide and rule

Sir Robert Naunton, who was born in 1563, wrote his *Fragmenta Regalia*, an account of Elizabeth and her courtiers and ministers, in the early years of Charles I's reign. He grasped one of the secrets of the Queen's success in government. Throughout her reign she made sure that no one man dominated her Council or monopolised her confidence. In this episode, however, either Bowyer was an inordinately bold man to ask the question he did or the story has much improved in the telling.

The principal note of . . . [Queen Elizabeth's] reign will be that she ruled much by faction and parties which herself both made, upheld, and weakened, as her own great judgment advised; for I dissent from the common received opinion that my lord of Leicester was absolute and above all in her grace . . . for proof whereof (among many that I could present) I will both relate a short and therein a known truth. And it was thus: Bowyer, a gentleman of the black-rod, being charged by her express command to look precisely to all admissions into the privy chamber, one day stayed a very gay captain and a follower of my lord of Leicester's from entrance, for that he was neither well known nor a sworn servant to the Queen. At which repulse the gentleman, bearing high on my lord's favour, told him he might perchance procure him a discharge. Leicester, coming into the contestation, said publicly . . . that he was a knave and should not continue long in his office; and so turning about to go into the Queen. Bowyer (who was a bold gentleman and well beloved) stepped before him and fell at her Majesty's feet, related the story, and humbly craves her Grace's pleasure and whether my lord of Leicester was King or her Majesty Queen. Whereunto she replied with her wonted oath (God's death!), my lord, I have wished you well but my favour is not so locked up for you that others shall not partake thereof; for I have many servants unto whom I have and will at my pleasure bequeath my favour and likewise resume the same. And if you think to rule here I will take a course to see you forthcoming. I will have here but one mistress and no master, and look that no ill happen to him, lest it be severely required at your hands; which so quelled my lord of Leicester that his feigned humility was long after one of his best virtues. . . .

R. Naunton, *Fragmenta Regalia* (1808), pp. 178–80

7   The work of the Council

In addition to its advisory duties the Privy Council was the highest administrative body in the realm, with the responsibility of supervising the whole field of government. This was an enormous task, but it also exercised judicial functions, and the determination of ordinary citizens to bring their cases before the most influential tribunal in the realm meant that it was pestered with private suits which interfered with its more important public functions. The orders of 1582 were an attempt to deal with this problem. They were repeated in 1589 and 1591, but seem to have had little practical effect. At the end of the reign the Council was still snowed under with private causes.

This day the Lords and others of her Majesty's Privy Council considering what multitude of matters concerning private causes and actions between party and party were daily brought unto the Council

Board, wherewith their Lordships were greatly troubled and her Majesty's special services oftentimes interrupted, for remedy whereof it was agreed among them that from henceforth no private causes arising between parties for any action whatsoever which may receive order and redress in any of her Majesty's ordinary courts shall be received and preferred to the Board, unless they shall concern the preservation of her Majesty's peace or shall be of some public consequence to touch the government of the realm.

15 April 1582, *Acts of the Privy Council*, New
Series, xiii, 394-5

8 As others see us

Guerau de Spes, Spanish ambassador to England from 1568 to 1572, was thoroughly inept and one of the least perceptive observers of the English political scene, as this account, written for his master Philip II, clearly demonstrates. His descriptions of the leading English councillors are little better than caricatures, but it is useful to remember that the Spanish government often had to frame its policy towards England on the basis of such misleading information from its envoys.

. . . The principal person in the Council at present is William Cecil, now Lord Burghley, a knight of the garter. He is a man of mean sort, but very astute, false, lying, and full of all artifice. He is a great heretic and such a clownish Englishman as to believe that all the Christian princes joined together are not able to injure the sovereign of his country, and he therefore treats their ministers with great arrogance.

This man manages the bulk of the business, and, by means of his vigilance and craftiness, together with his utter unscrupulousness of word and deed, thinks to outwit the ministers of other princes. This to a certain extent he has hitherto succeeded in doing. Next after him, the man who has most to do with affairs is Robert Dudley, earl of Leicester, not that he is fit for such work, but because of the great favour with which the Queen regards him. He is a light and greedy man who maintains the robbers and lives by their plunder. He is ungrateful for the favours your Majesty has granted to him and is greatly inclined to the French party, from whom he receives an allowance. The other man who has his hand in the government is the Lord Keeper, or guardian, as they call it, of the Great Seal [Sir Nicholas Bacon]. He is an obstinate and most malignant heretic, and, being Cecil's brother-in-law, always agrees with him. The Admiral [the earl of Lincoln] does not interfere very much in arranging matters, but

he is a very shameless thief, without any religion at all, which latter also
may be said of the earl of Sussex. The latter also belongs to the Council
and is a more capable man than any of the rest. He has shown signs
sometimes of wishing to serve your Majesty, as he is an enemy of the
earl of Leicester. The earl of Bedford also belongs to the Council. In
person and manners he is a monstrosity and a great heretic. There are
others of less authority than these men, lawyers, creatures of Cecil, who
only repeat what he says. They have recently admitted James Crofts
into the Council; he is secretly attached to the Catholic party and your
Majesty's service, but dares not speak very openly. . . .

> Account of 1571 by the Spanish ambassador
> De Spes regarding English affairs, *Cal. S.P.*
> *Spanish 1568–79*, p. 364

9   The Council divided

Throughout Elizabeth's reign the Privy Council was rent by faction—the
unanimity of the councillors in June 1562 was a very rare event—and the
greatest of all issues which divided the Council during the high Elizabethan
period was the question of whether or not to give open aid to the Dutch rebels
in their struggle against Spain. The three extracts which follow provide
evidence of these divisions between a 'peace party' headed by Burghley and a
'war party' led by Leicester with strong support from Sir Francis Walsingham,
who was secretary of state between 1573 and 1590. Although Burghley and his
supporters were in a minority on the Council their views prevailed for many
years because of the Queen's horror of the idea of war. It was only in 1585,
when it seemed that the Netherlands and perhaps all western Europe would be
brought under Spanish domination, that Elizabeth could be persuaded to send
open military aid to the Dutch rebels.

(i) . . . It is given out very maliciously amongst gentlemen and soldiers
and those of good sort who profess the religion that his lordship [i.e.
Burghley] has been the only let and overthrow of this Holland service,
by dissuading her Majesty from that enterprise, where otherwise the
earls of Leicester and Sussex were earnest furtherers of it. They judge
very hardly that the poor men being sent for by the Queen have been,
contrary to her promise, by indirect dealing so long delayed here to
their utter undoing at home and abroad. They say Mr. Walsingham
dealt justly with them in that he assured them from the beginning that
they would obtain nothing here, but lose their time. They say these
unworthy proceedings with foreign nations make the English the most
hated men in the world and to be condemned for mere abusers, as
those who put on religion, piety and justice for a cloak to serve

humours withal and please the time, while policy only is made both justice, religion and God with them.

William Herle to Lord Burghley, 14 March 1576, *Cal. S.P. Foreign Eliz. 1575-7*, pp. 269-70

(ii) . . . During the few days I have been here and in my conversations with the Queen I have found her much opposed to your Majesty's interests, as may be seen by the answers she has given me. And most of her ministers are quite alienated from us, particularly those who are most important, as, although there are seventeen councillors with the two secretaries, Hatton, and the new ones, the bulk of the business really depends upon the Queen, Leicester, Walsingham and Cecil, the latter of whom, although he takes part in the resolution of them by virtue of his office, absents himself on many occasions, as he is opposed to the Queen's helping the rebels so effectively and thus weakening her own position. He does not wish to break with Leicester and Walsingham on the matter, they being very much wedded to the States and extremely self-seeking, as I am assured that they are keeping the interest of the money which the Queen has lent to the States, without counting the presents they have received out of the principal. They urge the business under cloak of preserving their religion, which Cecil cannot well oppose, nor can he afford to make enemies of them, as they are well supported. Some of the councillors are well disposed towards your Majesty, but Leicester, whose spirit is Walsingham, is so highly favoured by the Queen, notwithstanding his bad character, that he centres in his hands and those of his friends most of the business of the country. . . .

Bernardino de Mendoza to King Philip II, 31 March 1578, *Cal. S.P. Spanish Elizabeth*, ii (1568-79), pp. 572-3

(iii) . . . Leicester, Hatton and Walsingham have endeavoured to persuade the Queen that it is desirable for her to openly take the States under her protection, as she could then settle with your Majesty on better terms, whereas, if she lets this opportunity pass, she can only look for ruin; because, if either your Majesty or Alençon and the French get possession of the country, neither one nor the other could be trusted. This view they have enforced by many arguments, but they have been opposed by Cecil and Sussex when the matter was discussed in the Council, and the question therefore remained undecided. When it was referred to the Queen, I understand that she complained greatly, saying what a miserable state was hers, since the death of a single person [i.e. the falsely rumoured death of the Prince of Orange] made all her councillors tremble and her subjects lose their courage.

> Bernardino de Mendoza to King Philip II,
> 25 April 1582, *Cal. S.P. Spanish Elizabeth*,
> (1580–86), iii, 346

10   A portrait of Lord Burghley

John Clapham, one of Burghley's clerks during the 1590s, left an accurate account of his master's influence. Burghley was not only the Queen's chief adviser but also the very lynch-pin of the administrative machine. As secretary of state between 1558 and 1572 and then as Lord Treasurer from 1572 until his death in 1598, he exercised tremendous power throughout the whole range of English administration. In addition, from 1561 onwards he was Master of the Court of Wards, an office which gave him a decisive voice in the distribution of an important part of the Queen's patronage. The principal accusation made against him by his contemporaries was that he concentrated power in himself and his followers by a self-interested use of his patronage.

About the fourteenth year of the Queen's reign Cecil was made Knight of the Garter, and, after the death of the Marquis of Winchester, Treasurer of England, he succeeded him in the treasurership, which office he enjoyed till his death; ordering the affairs of the realm in such a manner as he was respected even by his enemies, who reputed him the most famous councillor of Christendom in his time; the English government being then commonly termed by strangers Cecil's commonwealth....

In matters of counsel nothing for the most part was done without him, for that nothing was thought well done whereof he was not the contriver and director. His credit with the Queen was such as his wisdom and integrity well deserved. Howbeit..., he lived not always free from disgraces, which yet rather increased than diminished his estimation; for the necessity of his service would not any long time permit his absence from the Court and the greatness of his place procured him the envy of those who otherwise could not but acknowledge his virtues....

> J. Clapham, *Elizabeth of England*, ed. E.P. and
> C. Read (Philadelphia, 1951), pp. 76–7, 79

II   The Queen and Essex

Naunton's judgement on the career of Robert Devereux, Earl of Essex, the Queen's last favourite, reflects the delicate political situation at the end of her reign. Essex indeed may have believed that he could reduce the ageing Queen to a figurehead by placing his own supporters in the key offices in the state. Elizabeth resisted his importunities on behalf of his friends and gave the important offices of secretary of state (in 1596) and Master of the Wards (in 1599) to Sir Robert Cecil, but even so she tolerated Essex's incompetence and the difficulties of managing him until his revolt of 1601, which brought him to the scaffold. She was normally a superlative judge of men, but in the early stages Essex and the Queen misjudged each other. National hero though he was he paid with his life.

Sure it is that . . . [the earl of Essex] no sooner appeared in court but he took with the Queen and courtiers. . . . There was in this young lord, together with a most goodly person, a kind of urbanity or innate courtesy, which both won the Queen and too much took upon the people, to gaze upon the new adopted son of her favour. And as I go along it were not amiss to take into observation two notable quotations; the first was a violent indulgency of the Queen . . . towards this lord . . . , which argued a nonperpetuity; the second was a fault in the object of her grace, my lord himself, who drew in too fast, like a child sucking on an over-uberous nurse. And had there been a more decent decorum observed in both, or either of those, without doubt the unity of their affections had been more permanent, and not so in and out as they were, like an instrument ill tuned and lapsing to discord.

The great error of the two, though unwillingly, I am constrained to impose on my lord of Essex, or rather on his youth, and none of the least of his blame on those that stood sentinels about him, who might have advised him better, but that like men intoxicated with hopes they likewise had sucked in with the most and of their lord's receipt; and so like Caesar's would have all or none, a rule quite contrary to nature; and the most indulgent parents, who, though they may express more affection to one in the abundance of bequests, yet cannot forget some legacies, just distributives and dividends, to others of their begetting. And how hateful partiality proves every day's experience tells us, out of which common consideration might have framed to their hands a maxim of more discretion for the conduct and management of their now graced lord and master.

But . . . to do right to truth my lord of Essex, even of those that truly loved and honoured him, was noted for too bold an ingrosser, both of fame and favour. . . .

R. Naunton, *Fragmenta Regalia* (1808), pp. 267–70

12 Rivalry at Court

This report of 1595 by an envoy of the Duke of Württemberg provides evidence of the rivalry between Burghley and Essex. The former's own position was, of course, secure, but he was at that time trying to ensure the succession to high office of his son Robert Cecil in face of the intrigues of Essex and his supporters. As we have seen he succeeded in the following year, 1596, when the younger Cecil was appointed secretary of state.

. . . The gentlemen . . . at the English Court who are of the most consequence and through whose hands all matters must pass and to whom all foreign envoys have to apply are the earl of Essex, Grand Master of the Horse (who is at present deemed to be the Queen's sole favourite), and Lord Burghley, Lord Treasurer of England. This old gentleman can effect much with her Majesty. She does nothing or little without him, for he is, so to say, the Queen's code of laws. . . . I . . . learned that between the two aforesaid gentlemen the earl of Essex and the Lord Treasurer there obtained great jealousy and no little envy; wherefore frequently what the one was at pains to promote, the other thwarted with all his might. . . .

Report by Bruening von Buchenbach, envoy of the Duke of Württemberg in England, 1595, *Queen Elizabeth and some foreigners*, ed. V. von Klarwill, pp. 359, 362

13 Advice to a son

Burghley's advice to Robert Cecil, written in the 1580s, with its interesting comments on E (probably Essex) and R (almost certainly Raleigh), reflects something of the political perceptiveness of the old statesman. It is a judicious, and sententious, recipe for success in life.

8. Towards thy superiors be humble yet generous; with thy equals familiar yet respective; towards inferiors show much humility and some familiarity, as to bow thy body, stretch forth thy hand, and to uncover thy head, and suchlike popular compliments. The first prepares a way to advancement; the second makes thee known for a man well bred; the third gains a good report which once gotten may be

safely kept.... Yet do I advise thee not to affect nor to neglect popularity too much. Seek not to be E. and shun to be R.

Advice to a Son, ed. L. B. Wright (N.Y., 1962), pp. 12–13

14 The authority of parliament

In this famous passage, Sir Thomas Smith, experienced as diplomat, secretary of state, member of parliament, sets out the character and power of parliament. Note that his conception of representation does not necessarily include election. Elections rarely took place, since a patron would often nominate in the boroughs, or the local oligarchy would choose the members; while in the counties the election was often determined by agreement between factions. Apart from this, the majority of the inhabitants of a borough or county did not have the vote.

Where Smith talks of the authority of parliament, he means the king in parliament. Moreover, in spite of the very considerable powers he lists, the fact remains that parliament is essential only for legislation and taxation. If the crown does not need either, then parliament need not be assembled for years; and the crown alone determines when parliament should be summoned and dissolved. In the reign of Elizabeth I the equivalent to duration of parliament was three weeks per year. Many activities were outside the jurisdiction of parliament, notably the succession, foreign policy, the declaration of war and peace and—so the Queen claimed—ecclesiastical doctrine and practice.

The most high and absolute power of the realm of England consisteth in the parliament. For as in war where the king himself in person, the nobility, the rest of the gentility and the yeomanry are, is the force and power of England, so in peace and consultation where the prince is to give life and the last and highest commandment, the barony for the nobility and higher, the knights, squires, gentlemen and commons for the lower part of the commonwealth, the bishops for the clergy, be present to advertise consult and shew what is good and necessary for the commonwealth and to consult together, and upon mature deliberation every bill or law being thrice read and disputed upon in either house, the other two parts first each apart, and after the prince himself in presence of both the parties doth consent unto and alloweth. That is the prince's and whole realm's deed, whereupon justly no man can complain, but must accommodate himself to find it good and obey it.

That which is done by this consent is called firm, stable and *sanctum*. and is taken for law. The parliament abrogateth old laws, maketh new, giveth orders for things past, and for things hereafter to be followed, changeth rights and possessions of private men, legitimateth bastards, establisheth forms of religion, altereth weights and measures, giveth forms of succession to the Crown, defineth of doubtful rights whereof is no law already made, appointeth subsidies, tails, taxes, and impositions, giveth most free pardons and absolutions, restoreth in blood and name as the highest court, condemneth or absolveth them whom the prince will put to that trial. And, to be short, all that ever the people of Rome might do . . . the same may be done by the parliament of England, which representeth and hath the power of the whole realm both the head and the body. For every Englishman is intended to be there present, either in person or by procuration and attornies, of what preeminence, state, dignity or quality soever he be, from the prince (be he king or queen) to the lowest person of England. And the consent of the parliament is taken to be every man's consent.

> Of the parliament and the authority thereof,
> T. Smith, *De Republica Anglorum*, ed. Alston,
> pp. 48–9

15   A critic of parliamentary restraint

The redoubtable Peter Wentworth, an independent-minded, Puritan member is here challenging the crown's authority to prohibit parliament from initiating discussion on matters of state. Wentworth is at the same time protesting against the Speaker's control of debate in the crown interest. The Speaker, though formally elected by parliament, was a royal nominee. Wentworth himself died in the Tower.

Whether this Council [i.e. parliament] be not a place for any Member . . . freely and without controlment of any person or danger of law, by bill or speech to utter any . . . griefs . . . touching the service of God, the safety of the Prince and this noble Realm? . . . Whether it be not against the orders of this Council to make any secret or matter of weight which is here in hand known to the Prince or any other? . . . Whether the Speaker or any other may interrupt any member of this Council in his speech? . . . Whether the Speaker may rise when he will (any matter being propounded) without consent of the House? . . . Whether the Speaker may overrule the House? . . . Whether the Prince and State can . . . be maintained without this Council of Parliament, not altering the government of the State?

> Cited in J. E. Neale, *Elizabeth I and her Parliaments 1584–1601* (1957), p. 155

16 The Queen's defence

Through the Lord Keeper (i.e. Lord Chancellor, in everything but name) the Queen here defines the limits of parliamentary freedom of speech. These represent her pious hopes. They were frequently breached by radical Members.

. . . And albeit her Majesty hath evermore been most loath to call for the assembly of her people in parliament and hath done the same but rarely and only upon most just, weighty and great occasions tending directly to the honour of Almighty God, the maintenance of Christian religion and the needful defence thereof against the malicious and potent enemies of the same, so as she hath not either yearly as (for 17 years together) some of her progenitors, or otherwise not frequently, as all or the most of them have done, summoned the states of the land, though (upon turning the volumes of the laws and histories) it will easily appear that the causes occurring in the reign of her Majesty have been both more general and of more importance than those of former times, whereof a great many are but particular and not of the greatest moment, yet her most excellent Majesty would have you all to know that as of her own disposition she would yet still forbear as she hath done to draw you often together. So, nevertheless, considering the most weighty and urgent causes of this present time together with the great dangers threatened against her Majesty and her realms, which do not only continue but are since the last parliament in all appearance mightily grown and fearfully increased, her Majesty hath found it necessary that you should both understand of the same and also consider of time and fit remedy for the prevention and withstanding of them, the which also her Majesty trusteth that you will very carefully perform. . . .

. . . For liberty of speech her Majesty commandeth me to tell you that to say yea or no to bills, God forbid that any man should be restrained or afraid to answer according to his best liking, with some short declaration of his reason therein, and therein to have a free voice, which is the very true liberty of the House; not, as some suppose, to speak there of all causes as him listeth, and to frame a form of religion or a state of government as to their idle brains shall seem meetest. She sayeth no king fit for his state will suffer such absurdities. . . .

J. E. Neale, 'The Lord Keeper's speech to the parliament of 1592/3', *English Historical Review*, xxxi (1916), pp. 130, 136–7

17 The secretary of state

Though the great medieval office of the Lord Chancellor continued to be important, the growth and complexity of administration had vastly increased the role of the king's secretary, known from the sixteenth century onwards as the secretary of state. He was the most significant executive officer in both domestic and foreign affairs; the most important holders of the office were Thomas Cromwell under Henry VIII and William Cecil and later, his son Robert Cecil, under Elizabeth I. The office was frequently shared by two people.

All officers and counsellors of princes have a prescribed authority by patent, by custom, or by oath, the secretary only excepted; but, to the secretary, out of a confidence and singular affection, there is a liberty to negotiate at discretion at home and abroad, with friends and enemies, all matters of speech and intelligence.

All servants of princes deal upon strong and wary authority and warrant in disbursements as treasurers, in conference with enemies as generals, in commissions in executing offices by patent and instructions, and so in whatever else. Only a secretary hath no warrant or commission, no, not in matters of his own greatest particulars, but the virtue and word of his sovereign.

For such is the multiplicity of actions, and variable motions and intents of foreign princes and their daily practices, and in so many parts and places as secretaries can never have any commission so long and universal as to secure them.

So as a secretary must neither conceive the very thought of a king, which is only proper to God; or a king must exercise the painful office of a secretary, which is contrary to majesty and liberty; or else a prince must make choice of such a servant of such a prince, as the prince's assurance must be his confidence in the secretary, and the secretary's life his trust in the prince. . . .

As long as any matter, of what weight soever, is handled only between the prince and the secretary, those counsels are compared to the mutual affections of two lovers, undiscovered to their friends. . . .

> Robert Cecil, 'The state and dignity of a secretary of state's place', *Harleian Misc.*, ii, 281–2

18 The high cost of government

The cost of government was continually increasing as administration grew, the cost of living rose and wars and the preparation for war imposed heavy charges. All this meant that parliament had to be assembled to grant taxation, as called for in Lord Keeper Bacon's speech at the opening of parliament in 1559. The Queen's frugality held expenditure in check for the first two-thirds of the reign, but the outbreak of war with Spain in 1585 and the heavy drain of funds for the Irish struggle, left the crown financially weak at the end of the reign.

. . . But when a man looketh further, and considereth the marvellous decays and waste of the revenue of the crown, the inestimable consumption of the treasure levied both of the Crown and of the subject, the exceeding loss of munition and artillery, the great loss of divers valiant gentle men of very good service, the incredible sum of moneys owing at this present and in honour due to be paid, and the biting interest that is to be answered for the forbearance of this debt, therewith remembering the strength and mightiness of the enemy and his confederates, and how ready he is upon every occasion, upon every side, and in every time, to annoy you, and how the time most meet for that purpose draweth on at hand again. If a man consider the huge and most wonderful charge, newly grown to the Crown, more than ever hath heretofore been wont, and now of necessity to be continued. . . . Indeed I must confess that in those matters mine understanding is but small, and mine experience and time to learn, less. But in mine opinion this doth exceed the ancient yearly revenue of the crown.

> From Lord Keeper Nicholas Bacon's speech at the opening of the Queen's first Parliament, January 1559. D'Ewes, *The Journals of all the Parliaments* . . . (1682), p. 13

19 Where some of the money goes

The Queen's unwillingness to embark on an aggressive foreign policy had been a marked feature of her rule from her accession. After 1585, however, peace was not restored until 1604 in the new reign. The two excerpts which follow give very different views about the ultimate use of some of the heavy military expenditure. (The apparel of the common soldier is given later in the letter.)

(i) I must not forget nor cease to tell Her Majesty's good, wise, and gracious providings for us, her captains, and our soldiers, in summer heats and winter colds, in hunger and thirst, for our backs and our bellies: that is to say, every captain of an hundred footmen doth receive weekly, upon every Saturday, his full entertainment of twenty-eight shillings. In like case, every lieutenant fourteen shillings; an ensign, seven shillings; our sergeant, surgeon, drum and fife, five shillings pay, by way of imprest; and every common soldier, three shillings; delivered to all by the poll weekly. To the four last lower officers, two shillings weekly, and for every common soldier, twenty pence weekly, is to be answered to the full value thereof in good apparel of different kinds, part for winter, and part for summer, which is ordered of good quality and stuff for the prices; patterns whereof must be sent to the Lord Deputy to be compared and prepared as followeth:

Apparel for an officer in winter

A cassock of broad cloth, with baize, and trimmed with silk lace, 27 shillings and 7 pence.

A doublet of canvas with silk buttons, and lined with white linen, 14 shillings and 5 pence.

Two shirts and two bands, 9 shillings and 6 pence.

Three pair of kersey stockings, at 2 shillings and 4 pence per pair, 7 shillings.

Three pair of shoes of neat's leather at 2 shillings and 4 pence per pair, 7 shillings.

One pair of Venetians, of broad Kentish cloth, with silver lace, 15 shillings and 4 pence.

In summer

Two shirts and bands, 9 shillings 6 pence.

Two pair of shoes, 4 shillings 8 pence.

One pair of stockings, 2 shillings 8 pence.

A felt hat and band, 5 shillings 5 pence. . . .

> Letter of J. Harrington, *The Elizabethans*, ed.
> A. Nicoll (Cambridge, 1957), p. 139

(ii) The corruption of our wars springeth only from the rash and evil choice which hath best most commonly made of needy, riotous, licentious, ignorant, and base colonels, captains, lieutenants, sergeants, and such like officers, who have made merchandise of their places and without regard of their duty or respect of conscience have made port sale of their soldiers' blood and lives to maintain their unthriftiness and disorders.

> Henry Knyvett, Treatise on *The Defence of the*
> *Realme*, 1596, cited in *Shakespeare's England*, I,
> 121–2

20   Navy and privateers

The fundamental difference between the Royal Navy and the Merchant Navy had not yet emerged in sixteenth-century England. There was always a basic armed naval force but it was assumed that when necessary merchantmen could be armed and adapted for war conditions. At the same time privateers were at sea carrying letters of marque authorising them to stop and seize enemy ships, or neutral ships carrying munitions to the enemy. These ships were financed by investors—including ministers, in spite of what the Venetian Ambassador says in this passage—and sometimes considerable profits were made. But they disrupted trade and, in the long run, may have done more harm than good to England herself.

Whereas the Kings of England, down to Henry VII and Henry VIII, were wont to keep up a fleet of one hundred ships in full pay as a defence, now the Queen's ships do not amount to more than fifteen or sixteen, as her revenue cannot support a greater charge; and so the whole of the strength and repute of the nation rests on the vast number of small privateers, which are supported and increase to that dangerous extent which everyone recognises; and to ensure this suport, the privateers make the ministers partners in the profits, without the risk of a penny in the fitting out, but only a share in the prizes, which are adjudged by judges placed there by the ministers themselves.

C. G. Scaramelli, Report to Venice, 1603, *The Elizabethans*, ed. A. Nicoll (Cambridge, 1957), p. 142

21   Justice in action: King's Bench

The most important common law court for criminal offences was King's Bench, but comparable authority existed at the assizes, held twice a year in the shires before high court judges sent down from Westminster. Many criminal cases, however, were dealt with at quarter sessions by the justices of the peace. The processes could be complex and were strictly governed by highly technical principles. The following law report of a King's Bench case, dealt with in 1591, shows how an indictment could be quashed because it failed to use the appropriate term.

Penhall was indicted upon the statute of 5 E. 6 for drawing his dagger in the church against J.S. without saying that he drew it with intent to strike the party; and for that cause the indictment was holden void as to the statute. It was moved, if it should not be a good indictment for the assault, so as [i.e. that] he should be fined for the same. By Sands, Clerk of the Crown, and the whole Court, the indictment is void in all, for the conclusion of the indictment is *contra formam Statuti*, and then the jury cannot enquire at the common law.

Fourth Part of the Reports . . . of Cases (1675), ed.
W. Leonard, p. 49

22 Justice in action: the Star Chamber

Because of difficulties in enforcing the common law, sometimes for technical reasons as indicated in the preceding document, at other times because of the interference of over-mighty subjects and weaknesses of juries, the Star Chamber became a valuable prerogative court for bringing swift punishment to offenders. It was not established by a statute of 1487, as was once believed, but was part of the King's Council (with the addition of certain judges) sitting as a law court; nor was it restricted by common law procedures. In this report of a case of the year 1600, it is seen dealing firmly with a leading knight and some gentlemen involved in a breach of the peace.

Coke, the Queen's Attorney, informed by a bill on behalf of the Mayor, Aldermen and City of London against Sir Edmonde Baynam, knight, and Badger, Grauntam and Dutton, gentlemen, and Williamson, 'vintner in Bread Street' for riots and other misdemeanours in this manner: Sir Edmonde Baynam, Badger, Grauntam and Dutton went to supper in Bread Street at the 'Mermaid', where Williamson dwells and is a taverner, and there they supped and there they stayed until two 'a clock' in disorder and excess of drink; and then they departed with 'rapiers drawn', and menaced, wounded and beat the watch in Friday Street et in Paul's Churchyard, and did utter seditious words. But they confessed their faults and submitted themselves to the Court, and proved that all was done 'in drink and heat'. And for these misdemeanours each of them was fined £200 and imprisonment, but Williamson was acquitted by the sentence. Yet the Chief Justice, the Lord Treasurer and the Lord Keeper [would have] fined him £40 because he was *causa sine qua non*. But because he was known [to be] an honest man and of good government, and would not suffer music and illegal games in his house, and sent for the constable for [to keep] good order, he was acquitted by the sentence. . . .

Les Reportes del Cases in Camera Stellata, 1593
to 1609, ed. W. P. Baildon (1894), p. 114

23   Justice in action: treason

The Tudor period is widely spoken of as a time when the 'rule of law' was being established throughout the realm. This passage from Harrison gives some measure of its severity against enemies of the state at a time when England, like every European state, was conscious of the many grave threats to order. It should, however, be added that English law was in many respects less severe than elsewhere in Europe; and that the royal pardon was sometimes extensively used to ameliorate the law.

The greatest and most grievous punishment used in England, for such as offend against the state, is drawing from the prison to the place of execution upon an hardle or sled, where they are hanged till they be half dead, and then taken down and quartered alive; after that their members and bowels are cut from their bodies and thrown into a fire provided near hand and within their own sight, even for the same purpose. Sometimes, if the trespass be not the more heinous, they are suffered to hang till they be quite dead. And whensoever any of the nobility are convicted of high treason by their peers . . . this manner of their death is converted into the loss of their heads only, notwithstanding that the sentence do run after the fomer order. In trial of cases concerning treason, felony or any other grievous crime not confessed, the party accused doth yield, if he be a nobleman, to be tried by . . . his peers; if a gentleman by gentlemen; and an inferior by God and by the country, to wit, the yeomanry (for combat or battle is not greatly in use) and being condemned of felony, manslaughter, etc., he is oftsoons hanged by the neck till he be dead, and then cut down and buried. But if he be convicted of wilful murder, done either upon pretended malice or in any notable robbery, he is either hanged alive in chains near the place where the fact was committed or else, upon compassion taken, first strangled with a rope, and so continueth till his bones consume to nothing. We have use neither of the wheel nor of the bar, as in other countries, but when wilful manslaughter is perpetrated, beside hanging the offender hath his right hand commonly stricken off before or near unto the place where the act was done, after which he is led forth to the place of execution, and there put to death according to the law. . . .

If a woman poison her husband she is burned alive; if the servant kill his master he is to be executed for petty treason; he that poisoneth a man is to be boiled to death in water or lead, although the party die not of the practise. In cases of murder all the accessaries are to suffer pains of death accordingly. Perjury is punished by the pillory, burning in the forehead with the letter P . . . , and loss of all his moveables. Many trespasses also are punished by the cutting of one or both ears from the head of the offender, as the utterance of seditious words against the magistrates. . . . Rogues are burned through the ears; carriers of sheep out of the land by the loss of their hands; such as kill by poison are either boiled or scalded to death in lead or seething water. Heretics are burned quick; harlots and their mates by carting, ducking, and doing of open penance in sheets . . . are often put to rebuke. . . .

W. Harrison, *Description of England*, ed. F. J. Furnivall (1877), i, 222–5

24 Local administration: the justice of the peace

The power of the Privy Council never fully measured up to its claims and part of the explanation was its weakness in provincial administration. The sheriff, though still important, had lost his military importance to the commission of muasters and the Lord Lieutenancy; while social administration and the maintenance of order were essentially the responsibility of the justices of the peace. They were drawn from the local gentry and met four times a year in the county, where they acted as a common law court as well as transacted their administrative business, dealing with roads, poor law and other matters. The justices—who received the by now nominal fee of 4s. per day—were in most cases amateurs, though some had spent a year or two at one of the Inns of Court; and they were subject to local influences and pressures. And where their interests conflicted with those of the government, central policy could be ignored or subverted. The government could retaliate by dismissing them and summoning them before the Privy Council.

William Lambarde the author of this passage was the famous Kent antiquary, topographer and lawyer.

As justice cannot be administered without both a declaration of the law and an execution of the same, so to the end that our justices of the peace may be able to deliver justice they are accomplished with double power, the one of jurisdiction and the other of coercion; that is to say, with ample authority not only to convent the persons but also (after the cause heard and adjudged) to constrain them to the obedience of their order and decree.

This jurisdiction of theirs is exercised for the most part (if not altogether) about those causes which be in a manner the same that the civil lawyers do call *iudicia publica*, partly because the prince (who representeth the head of the commonwealth) hath interest in the most of them, as well as that private person which is immediately offended;

and partly because they are not commonly tried by such action as other civil and private causes are, but rather by criminal and public accusation, information or presentment. . . .

But if the authority of these justices should cease when the fault is told, heard and adjudged, then should they be no better than half justices; and therefore the law hath also put coercion, execution or punishment (as I said) into their hands lest otherwise their judgements should be deluded for want of power to bring them to effect.

This punishment then is an orderly execution of a lawful judgement laid upon an offender by the minister of the law. And it is done for four causes; first, for the amendment of the offender; secondly, for examples sake, that others may be thereby kept from offending; thirdly, for the maintenance of the authority and credit of the person that is offended; and these three reasons be common to all such punishments. Seneca rehearseth the fourth, final cause; that is to say that (wicked men being taken away) the good may live in better security: and this pertaineth not to all, but to capital punishments only, as every man may at the first hearing understand. . . .

The punishments that be commonly put in execution at this day and wherewith the justices of the peace have to do, they be divided into coporal, pecuniary and infamous.

Corporal punishment is either capital or not capital. Capital (or deadly) punishment is done sundry ways as by hanging, burning, boiling or pressing. Not capital is of divers sorts also, as cutting off the hand or ear, burning (or marking) the hand or face, whipping, imprisoning, stocking, setting on the pillory, or cuckingstool, which in old time was called the tumbrel. . . .

Under the name of pecuniary punishment I comprehend all issues, fines, amercements, and forfeitures of offices, goods or lands.

And if the justices of peace may by virtue of their commission deal with such conspirators as do confederate together to cause any person unjustly to be indicted of felony, whereof afterward he is acquitted (as some do think they may), then is there a special punishment in that case appointed by law, which . . . is termed villanous and may be well called infamous, because the judgement in such case shall be like unto the ancient judgement in attaint . . . and is . . . set down to be that their oaths shall not be of any credit after, nor lawful for them in person to approach the Queen's courts, and that their lands and goods be seized into the Queen's hands, their trees rooted up, and their bodies imprisoned etc. And at this day the punishment appointed for perjury (having somewhat more in it than coporal or pecuniary pain), stretching to the discrediting of the testimony of the offender for ever after, may be partaker of this name.

W. Lambarde, *Eirenarcha* (1599 ed.), pp. 60–63

25   The government and the justices

The following extract indicates the kind of communication passing between the government and an influential local justice, Sir Nathaniel Bacon. The first complaint refers to disorderly behaviour in general, attributed to an excess of alehouses, a frequent cause of government criticism. The second concerns special episodes, so serious as to call for trial at the Assizes.

With my very hearty commendations. You shall receive herewith two several complaints. The one concerning certain unnecessary alehouses in the town of Cromer and sundry disorders committed in and by reason of the same. The other touching an outrage done (if it be true) in very riotous manner at Antingham by divers named in the same petition. Because the same may not pass away without due examination I have thought good hereby to pray you to call the parties before you and to examine the causes contained in these two several complaints exactly and thereupon (sufficient cause appearing) to bind the offenders with good sureties to make their personal appearance at the next Assizes for the county of Norfolk to answer the same, and then to certify me of your proceedings herein. . . .

Lord Chief Justice Sir John Popham to Nathaniel Bacon, 4 February 1602, *The Official Papers of Sir Nathaniel Bacon of Stiffkey, Norfolk, Camden Soc.*, 3rd ser., xxvi (1915), pp. 52–3

26   Two views on the justices

In their response to Privy Council directions the justices of the peace of Norfolk report, in 1586, the efforts that they have made to maintain supplies of food and keep down prices. The rebuke administered to them on a later occasion (ii, below) by the Privy Council indicates either slackness on their part, or that the problem is intractable. Certainly in times of acute scarcity the problem could not be solved by administrative action.

(i) May it please your honours, after the remembrance of our humble duties to be advertised; that for a further proceeding in the accomplishment of your honourable letters concerning the furnishing of the markets with corn, we have according to our former letters of the 9th of June last met here together this day for conference therein. And perusing all our notes and proceedings together, we find that throughout this shire by such order as we have taken with owners and farmers and also badgers and buyers of corn and grain, the markets are by them plentifully served every market day with corn, and the same sold at reasonable rates, viz., wheat at 22/– the quarter, rye at 16/–, malt at 14/–, and barley at 12/–, of which kinds of corn the poorer sort are by persuasion served at meaner prices. And so we doubt not but it shall likewise continue according to our direction until it shall please God that new corn may be used. And hereof thinking it best in performance of our duties to advertise your honours, we humbly take our leave. From Attlebridge the 11th of July 1586.

> Report of justices of the peace to the Privy Council concerning scarcity in Norfolk, 1586, in *English Economic History, Select Documents,* ed. Bland, Brown and Tawney, pp. 373–4

(ii) After our hearty commendations, whereas you received letters from us eight months since to make careful and present enquiry and certificate of all the full numbers and quantities of provisions taken for Her Majesty's house and stable and therein signified the great and gracious care Her Majesty hath for the reformation of great abuses committed by purveyors to her Highness' subjects. And for that we understand not of any performance by you of this her Majesty's commandment and pleasure, whereas [sic] we greatly marvel, considering the usual complaints made in Parliament. We do therefore again will and require you in her Majesty's name that presently you do proceed to the diligent execution and performance of the full effect of the same our former letters. And for the better effecting thereof that you do swear four or six honest substantial men of every parish, that they do examine and receive true certificate of every person in their parish, what numbers and quantities of provisions have been in that time of two years past taken from thence either at their houses or grounds or in any fair of market or elsewhere, with the purveyors' names that took the same and from whom, at what time in the year, and for what price, and what remaineth due for any provisions taken, and as further is expressed in our former letters. And that with all speed you send us the said certificates that you may make some part of satisfaction for you slackness past. And that we may know from you all the divisions within your shire and the justices' names that dwell therein, thereby to understand who they be that make default in not performing her Highness' pleasure in our letters expressed. . . .

> The Privy Council to the sheriff and justices of the peace of Norfolk, 26 February 1591. *The Official Papers of Nathaniel Bacon*, ed. H. W. Saunders, Camden Soc., 3rd series, xxv (1915), pp. 64–5

27 Jobbery

Tudor government was personal government. Though all appointments to office went through an official machine, in fact the links were personal and advancement depended in part on ability and in part on having the right contact in the right place. One well-known 'contact-man' was Michael Hickes, personal assistant to Lord Burghley and, after him, to his son Robert Cecil. Such applications for office as went through him were often accompanied by the promise, or hint, of a gift, as is indicated by the two extracts given below.

(i) Mr. Hickes, our very hearty commendations remembered. Understanding by the bringer hereof John Lewes, our town clerk, your readiness and willingness in preferring and furthering such petitions and suits as the last term he had cause for us in our names to prefer to the right honourable our very good lord the Lord High Treasurer of England, we have therefore thought it our part not only to yield unto you our hearty thanks for the same, but also earnestly to desire continuance of that your great courtesy and friendship, for which you shall be assured both to find us thankful and also ready to the uttermost of our powers to do any pleasure to you or any your friends as opportunity anyway may serve. . . .

> The mayor and burgesses of Hull to Michael Hickes, 28 April 1590, B.M. Lansd. MS. 64 f. 92r

(ii) Good Mr. Hickes, I understand by this bearer Isaac Burgis, a gentleman of her Majesty's chapel, that he hath been an humble suitor to my Lord Treasurer for the escheator's office of Sussex and Surrey and was in good hope and possibility by his honourable favour to obtain the same if he had brought him the commendations of the justices of assize of the country, whereby his lordship might understand that he had been a sufficient man for such an office. And for that I long since knew him to be one of my Lord Dyer's clerks and that for his skill and sufficiency my Lord Dyer preferred him to a filazer's office of the Common Pleas for the shires of Kent, Sussex and Surrey, and that office he honestly and sufficiently executed, and, since my Lord Dyer's death hath for the better service of her Majesty in her chapel given over the same; which place and office he could not have supplied had he not been thought by all the judges of Common Pleas to be honest, skilful, and sufficient. And therefore I thought good at his request to certify you so much and that I think him to be a fit and skilful man to supply the office of an escheator, and so pray you, if need be, to inform my lord; and that this gentleman may have your friendly assistance herein, who for his part will not be unmindful of your favour therein. And I shall think myself beholding to you, for that it is for one whom my Lord Dyer was greatly beholding. . . .

> Baron Matthew Ewens to Michael Hickes,
> November 1594, B.M. Lansd. MS. 77 f. 178r

28 The perils of being a courtier

The Elizabethan Court was not simply the gay, glamorous place of romantic history. It was also the centre of government where power was held and manipulated; and to gain office there involved tremendous and bitter competition. It could also be highly expensive, as these two extracts illustrate. The first comes from Walter Mildmay's advice to his son, the second from a collection of Francis Bacon's apophthegms, published after his death.

(i) Know the Court but spend not thy life there, for Court is a very chargeable place. I would rather wish thee to spend the greatest part of thy life in the country than to live in this glittering misery.

> Cited in Joan Simon, *Education and Society in Tudor England* (Cambridge, 1966), p. 352

(ii) In eighty-eight, when the queen went from Temple-bar along Fleet St. the lawyers were ranked on one side, and the companies of the city on the other. Said Master Bacon to a lawyer that stood next him: 'Do but observe the courtiers: if they bow first to the citizens, they are in debt; if first to us, they are in law.'

> *The Works of Francis Bacon* (1859), ed.
> J. Spedding, *et. al.*, vii, 175

29 The abuse of power

The Lie has been quoted earlier (Document no. **III, 8**) in its comment on education. Here the poet attacks the corruption which, he says, is found throughout the upper ranks of Church and State.

> Say to the Court it glows,
> And shines like rotten wood,
> Say to the Church it shows
> What's good, and doth no good.
> If Church and Court reply,
> Then give them both the lie.
>
> Tell potentates they live
> Acting by others' action,
> Not loved unless they give,
> Not strong but by affection.
> If potentates reply,
> Give potentates the lie.
>
> Tell men of high condition
> That manage the estate,
> Their purpose is ambition,
> Their practice only hate.
> And if they once reply
> Then give them all the lie.
>   W. Raleigh, *The Lie*

SUGGESTIONS FOR FURTHER READING

Elizabethan People:

F. Aydelotte, *Elizabethan Rogues and Vagabonds* (Oxford, 1913)

B. W. Beckingsale, *Elizabeth I* (1963)

S. T. Bindoff, *Tudor England* (1950)

Mildred Campbell, *The English Yeoman under Elizabeth I and the Early Stuarts* (New Haven, 1942)

Mary A. Finch, *The Wealth of Five Northamptonshire Families, 1540–1640* (Oxford, 1956)

J. Hurstfield, *Elizabeth I and the Unity of England* (1960)

W. K. Jordan, *Philanthropy in England, 1480–1660* (New York, 1959)

E. M. Leonard, *The Early History of English Poor Relief* (Cambridge, 1900)

W. T. MacCaffrey, *Exeter, 1540–1640* (Cambridge, Mass., 1958)

K. Muir and S. Schoenbaum (eds.), *A New Companion to Shakespeare Studies* (1971)

J. E. Neale, *Queen Elizabeth* (1934)

D. B. Quinn, *Raleigh and the British Empire* (1947)

A. L. Rowse, *The England of Elizabeth* (1950)

J. F. D. Shrewsbury, *A History of Bubonic Plague in the British Isles,* (Cambridge, 1970)

L. Stone, *The Crisis of the Aristocracy, 1558–1641* (Oxford, 1965)

The Economy:

P. J. Bowden, *The Wool Trade in Tudor and Stuart England* (1962)

D. C. Coleman, 'Industrial Growth and Industrial Revolutions', *Economica*, February 1956

W. G. Hoskins, 'Harvest Fluctuations and English Economic History, 1480–1619', *Agricultural History Review*, xii (1964)

E. Kerridge, *Agrarian Problems in the Sixteenth Century and After* (1969)

J. U. Nef, *The Rise of the British Coal Industry* (2 vols., 1932)

R. B. Outhwaite, *Inflation in Tudor and Early Stuart England* (1969)

P. Ramsey, *Tudor Economic Problems* (1966)

R. H. Tawney, *The Agrarian Problem in the Sixteenth Century* (Harper Torchbooks ed., with introduction by Lawrence Stone, New York, 1967)

Joan Thirsk (ed.), *The Agrarian History of England and Wales*, vol. iv, *1500–1640* (Cambridge, 1967)

Joan Thirsk, *Tudor Enclosures* (Historical Association Pamphlet, 1959)

T. S. Willan, *Studies in Elizabethan Foreign Trade* (Manchester, 1959)

T. Wilson, *A Discourse upon Usury*, ed. R. H. Tawney (New York, 1925)

Intellectual Developments:

J. Buxton, *Sir Philip Sidney and the English Renaissance* (1954)

E. K. Chambers, *William Shakespeare* (2 vols., Oxford, 1930)

K. Charlton, *Education in Renaissance England* (Toronto, 1965)

W. S. C. Copeman, *Doctors and Disease in Tudor Times* (1960)

M. H. Curtis, *Oxford and Cambridge in Transition, 1558–1642* (Oxford, 1959)

F. R. Johnson, *Astronomical Thought in Renaissance England* (Baltimore, 1937)

W. K. Jordan, *Philanthropy in England, 1480–1660* (New York, 1959)

C. S. Lewis, *English Literature in the Sixteenth Century, excluding Drama* (Oxford, 1954)

Eleanor Rosenberg, *Leicester, Patron of Letters* (New York, 1955)

L. V. Ryan, *Roger Ascham* (Stanford, 1963)

F. S. Siebert, *Freedom of the Press in England, 1476–1776* (Urbana, 1965)

Joan Simon, *Education and Society in Tudor England* (Cambridge, 1966)

C. S. Singer, *et al.*, *A History of Technology*, vol. iii (Oxford, 1957)

L. Stone, 'The Educational Revolution in England, 1560–1640', *Past and Present*, July 1964

E. M. W. Tillyard, *The Elizabethan World Picture* (1943)
W. P. D. Wightman, *Science and the Renaissance*, vol. i (1962)

Religion:

J. E. Booty (ed.), *An Apology of the Church of England* (Ithaca, 1963)
J. Bossy, 'The Character of Elizabethan Catholicism', *Past and Present*, April 1962
V. J. K. Brook, *Archbishop Parker* (Oxford, 1962)
V. J. K. Brook, *Whitgift and the English Church* (1957)
P. Collinson, *The Elizabethan Puritan Movement* (1967)
Claire Cross, *The Royal Supremacy in the Elizabethan Church* (1969)
A. G. Dickens, *The English Reformation* (1964)
C. Hill, *Economic Problems of the Church from Archbishop Whitgift to the Long Parliament* (Oxford, 1956)
R. Hooker, *Of the Laws of Ecclesiastical Polity* (Everyman ed., with introduction by Christopher Morris, 2 vols., 1964-5)
P. McGrath, *Papists and Puritans under Elizabeth I* (1967)
J. E. Neale, 'The Elizabethan Acts of Supremacy and Uniformity', *English Historical Review*, lxv (1950)

Government and Administration:

L. Boynton, *The Elizabethan Militia* (1967)
E. P. Cheyney, *History of England*, vol. i (1914)
C. G. Cruickshank, *Elizabeth's Army* (2nd ed., Oxford, 1966)
F. C. Dietz, *English Public Finance, 1558–1641* (New York, 1932)
G. R. Elton, *The Tudor Constitution* (Cambridge, 1960)
F. M. G. Evans, *The Principal Secretary of State* (Manchester, 1923)
W. S. Holdsworth, *History of English Law*, vol. i (1923, 7th ed., 1956), vols. iv, v (3rd ed., 1924)
J. Hurstfield, 'County government, c. 1530–c. 1660', *The Victoria History of the Counties of England: Wiltshire*, v, (1957)
J. Hurstfield, *The Queen's Wards* (1958)
W. J. Jones, *The Elizabethan Court of Chancery* (Oxford, 1967)
W. T. MacCaffrey, 'Place and Patronage in Elizabethan Politics', *Elizabethan Government and Society*, eds. S. T. Bindoff, J. Hurstfield, C. H. Williams (1961)

W. T. MacCaffrey, *The Shaping of the Elizabethan Regime* (1969)

C. Morris, *Political Thought in England, Tyndale to Hooker* (1953)

J. E. Neale, *Elizabeth I and her Parliaments* (2 vols., 1953, 1957)

J. E. Neale, *The Elizabethan House of Commons* (1949)

J. E. Neale, *Essays in Elizabethan History* (1958)

M. Oppenheim, *A History of the Administration of the Royal Navy* (1898)

C. Read, *Mr. Secretary Cecil and Queen Elizabeth* (1955)

C. Read, *Lord Burghley and Queen Elizabeth* (1960)

C. Read, *Mr. Secretary Walsingham* (3 vols., Oxford, 1925)

C. S. Russell, *The Crisis of Parliaments* (1971)

Gladys Scott Thomson, *Lords Lieutenant in the Sixteenth Century* (1923)

A. G. R. Smith, *The Government of Elizabethan England* (1967)

P. Williams, *The Council in the Marches of Wales under Elizabeth I* (Cardiff, 1958)

T